Crafting with
GOURDS

D1067119

Crafting with GOURDS

Building, Painting, and Embellishing Birdhouses, Flowerpots, Wind Chimes, and More

Lora S. Irish

FOX CHAPEL
PUBLISHING

Acknowledgements

I wish to extend my deepest thanks to Chris Reggio, Tiffany Hill, Colleen Dorsey, and Wendy Reynolds for their excellent work in creation, development, and refinement of this manuscript. As an author, it is a wonderful experience to be working with such a well-skilled team.

© 2018 by Lora S. Irish and Fox Chapel Publishing Company, Inc., 903 Square Street, Mount Joy, PA 17552.

Crafting with Gourds is an original work, first published in 2018 by Fox Chapel Publishing Company, Inc. The patterns contained herein are copyrighted by the author. Readers may make copies of these patterns for personal use. The patterns themselves, however, are not to be duplicated for resale or distribution under any circumstances. Any such copying is a violation of copyright law.

Shutterstock photos: pages 8–9 gourds by KobchaiMa; page 22 brushes by Kostenko Maxim; page 25 painter's tape by Mega Pixel; page 27 gloves by Looka; pages 46–47 paints by Angela Ostafichuk; pages 130–131 textiles by Marta Maziar.

ISBN 978-1-56523-960-9

Library of Congress Cataloging-in-Publication Data

Names: Irish, Lora S., author.
Title: Crafting with gourds / Lora S. Irish.
Description: Mount Joy : Fox Chapel Publishing, [2018] | Includes index. |
  Identifiers: LCCN 2018028217 (print) | LCCN 2018031682 (ebook) | ISBN
  9781607655503 (ebook) | ISBN 9781565239609
Subjects: LCSH: Gourd craft.
Classification: LCC TT873.5 (ebook) | LCC TT873.5 .I75 2018 (print) | DDC
  745.5—dc23
LC record available at https://lccn.loc.gov/2018028217

To learn more about the other great books from Fox Chapel Publishing, or to find a retailer near you, call toll-free 800-457-9112 or visit us at *www.FoxChapelPublishing.com*.

We are always looking for talented authors. To submit an idea, please send a brief inquiry to acquisitions@foxchapelpublishing.com.

Printed in Singapore
First printing

Because working with gourds and other materials inherently includes the risk of injury and damage, this book cannot guarantee that creating the projects in this book is safe for everyone. For this reason, this book is sold without warranties or guarantees of any kind, expressed or implied, and the publisher and the author disclaim any liability for any injuries, losses, or damages caused in any way by the content of this book or the reader's use of the tools needed to complete the projects presented here. The publisher and the author urge all readers to thoroughly review each project and to understand the use of all tools before beginning any project.

Introduction

Gourds are beautiful, dynamic, organic items that are a joy to use in crafting. You can construct interesting and useful shapes with gourds and then paint and decorate them in unique and interesting ways. The projects that you will encounter in this book can be used as fully finished standalone pieces or as bold, bright backgrounds for your own patterns and designs. The techniques you will learn are so versatile that you can use gourds of any shape or size and then put those gourds to many uses—as flowerpots, soap dishes, birdhouses, decorations, or whatever else you can imagine.

You will be creatively manipulating color by using plastic straws, sea sponges, plastic netting, and old toothbrushes. You will be dripping color, dabbing color, splattering color, and sponging color into dynamic, free-flowing mixes. You will also learn how to add and control texture in your gourd art by working with air-dry modeling clay, acrylic sculpture paste, and collage using burlap, twine, and even newspaper.

So grab your stash of gourds, set out all your painting supplies, pull a chair up to your worktable, and get ready to have fun crafting with gourds.

There are no detailed step-by-step instructions for these little owls in this book, but by the time you have worked on the other projects, you will be ready to create them on your own using your new gourd art skills.

118

86

132

58

74

100

146

154

158

Contents

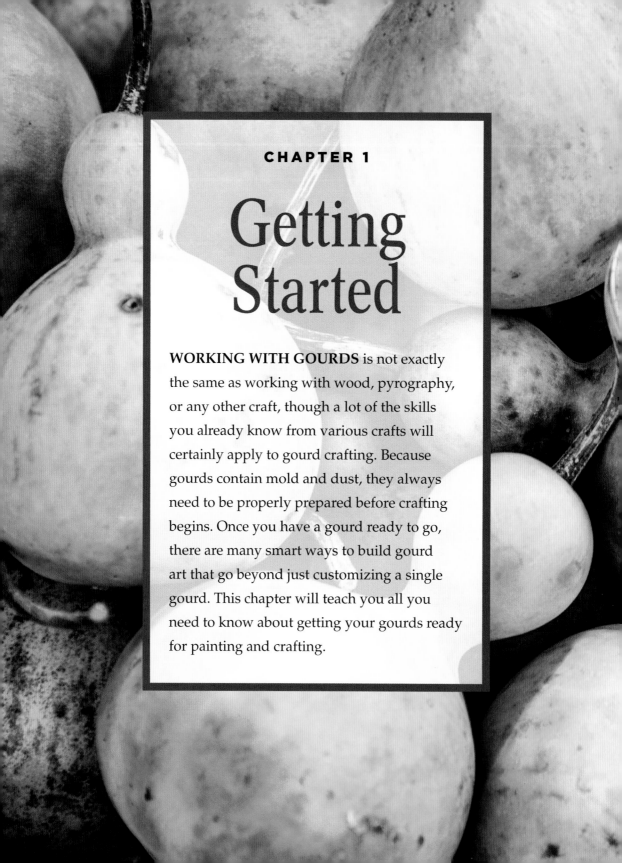

CHAPTER 1

Getting Started

WORKING WITH GOURDS is not exactly the same as working with wood, pyrography, or any other craft, though a lot of the skills you already know from various crafts will certainly apply to gourd crafting. Because gourds contain mold and dust, they always need to be properly prepared before crafting begins. Once you have a gourd ready to go, there are many smart ways to build gourd art that go beyond just customizing a single gourd. This chapter will teach you all you need to know about getting your gourds ready for painting and crafting.

Thinking about Gourd Projects

Examine the Gourd

A few moments of preparation early on can save you hours of struggle later in your gourd project. Take time to check your gourd for both its best features and its problem areas. Remember that what may appear at first to be a major problem can often be turned to your advantage if you prepare in advance.

Feature	Solution
Uneven bottom	Better hanging than sitting
Pits and holes	Open with a knife and fill with sculpture paste
Scarring	Sand with 220-grit sandpaper
Nice, straight neck	Excellent for a birdhouse
Fat, round belly	Lots of room for a nest
Blotchy color	Use a primer

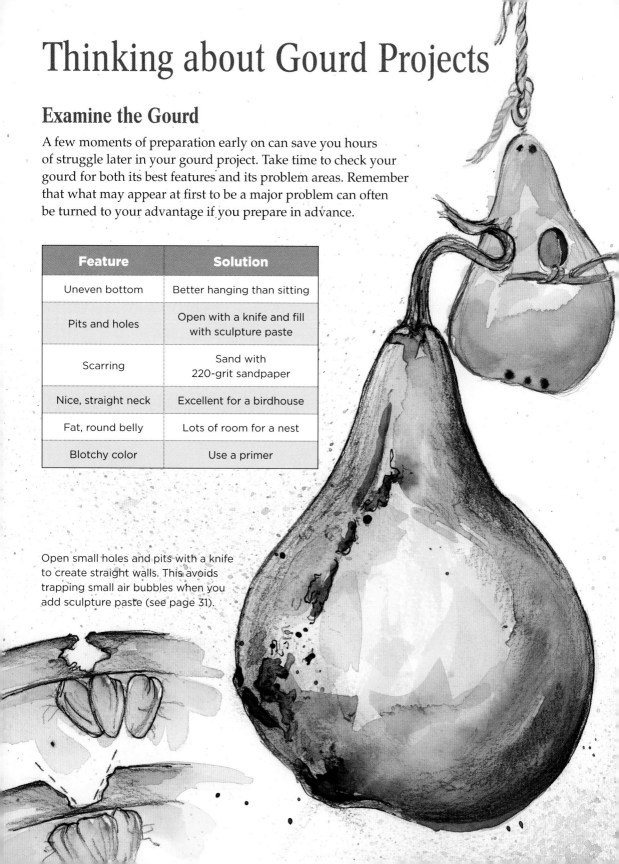

Open small holes and pits with a knife to create straight walls. This avoids trapping small air bubbles when you add sculpture paste (see page 31).

Plan the Structure

By planning first where you need to add hardware, holes, and accents to your project, you can determine exactly how much space you actually have for your artistic design. Here's an example birdhouse plan including all its features. The decorative design will need to be customized to suit these features.

- Vent holes at top for air circulation

- Drainage holes at bottom

- Placement of perch/perch holes

- Added eye hook using wood filler

- Thinner neck tucks into the leaves of the branch

- Size and placement of the hole determines the kind of bird that will nest here

Plot the Design

A quick pencil sketch can help you plot your focus points, accent elements, and the overall shape of your design. With colored pencils, crayons, or gel pens, you can lay out the general color areas inside your pattern, too. It is far easier to make adjustments and changes on paper than it is when you are in the midst of painting.

- A bright focal area just below the nesting hole brings the eye to where there will be activity in the nest.

- A blue to blue-green wash background will intensify the yellows and oranges in the poppies.

- Small purple violets complement the orange of the poppy flowers, yet blend with the bluish background.

- Branches of three to five leaves will help the design curl around the sides of the gourd.

Supplies

Brushes

For most painting, you'll need some kind of brush. The bristles of a brush determine how the brush can and should be used in a project. Stiff-bristled brushes are used to scrub the paint into the deep crevices of a piece, whereas very soft-bristled, flexible brushes hold large amounts of color and are used to flood an area with paint. Natural-haired brushes have a spring action that helps create thin, long, controllable line work. Below is a review of a few key kinds of brush bristle types. Brush shape is also relevant to painting—see pages 14–15 for more detail.

A Extremely soft, thin bristles, whether natural or synthetic, are used to hold large amounts of color with each brushstroke. This type of bristle is most commonly found in mop brushes and is used to flood an area with thinned color.

B Ox-hair blends, as shown in this deer-foot stippler brush, are a stiff, firm bristle that has little bend or spring. When applying color, the blended ox-hair bristles hold the shape of the brush's profile.

C Ox-hair brushes are created from goat or pig hair. They are strong and stiff, allowing you to scrub color into tight, deep crevices. Use an ox-hair brush when you want overall coverage of a color that will have no spaces with small, trapped air bubbles. These brushes are most commonly used for primer coats, full coverage coats, and oil stains.

D Red synthetic bristles give you the flexibility of a natural-haired brush, similar to a red sable (see F), but without the high price. The flat shaders, rounds, and liners that use a red synthetic bristle are the mainstay of our brush kit, used to fill areas and create shaded strokes.

E White synthetic bristles are softer and more flexible than red synthetic bristles, similar to a squirrel-hair bristle (see G). White synthetics, available in flat shader, round, and liner styles, create extra-smooth brushstrokes and are wonderful for wash techniques.

F Red sables are natural bristles that carry a large amount of color. Sables have a natural spring, returning the brush to a fine point or fine edge as you push and then lift the brush off the project.

G Squirrel-hair bristles are extra-soft, natural bristles that hold their shape and spring even with very hard use. This bristle type gives the greatest range of flexibility to your brushstroke work.

Regarding brush shape, there are many different brush shapes that each have different best uses. Here is a brief tour of seven different shapes you may want to use and that are used throughout this book.

Fan brushes are perfect for applying thinned wash coats and creating interesting texture strokes. The wide, curved edge disguises the beginning of the brushstrokes so that the color application easily blends into one even coating.

Mops can have either flat or curved leading edges. The three brushes pictured are all flat mops. Whether their bristles are synthetic or natural, these brushes have soft, springy hair that allows the brush to hold enormous quantities of color. As their name implies, mops are used to apply thinned wash coats of color.

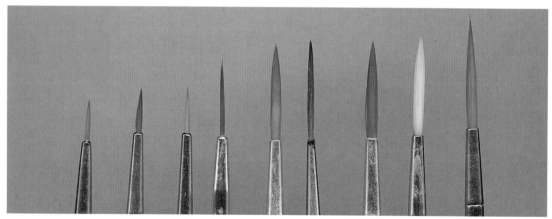

Liners are used to create fine line details in your work. Smaller liners, numbered from the small #000 through the large #1, are often called fine liners, China liners, or China dolls, as they were originally designed to paint the fine eyelashes and eyebrows on ceramic doll faces. These sizes are usually ½" (1cm) long or shorter. Longer liners, shown middle, which begin at around 1" (2.5cm) long, are sized from #2 up to size #24. This style of brush has extra-long bristles for maximum paint capacity that come to an extra-sharp point. The #4 liner, shown far right in this photo, can create a finer line than the three left fine liners at far left, and that line can be over 12" (30.5cm) long per brushful of color.

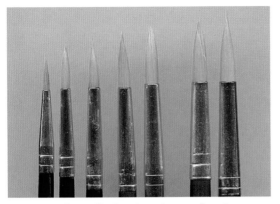

Rounds, also called pointed rounds, give you the advantage of the fine point found in liners but with the addition of a wider body that has a higher paint capacity. This style of brush is used for full coverage and for specialty brushstrokes that create shaded petals, leaves, and calligraphy strokes. Sizes for rounds are not standardized and so may vary between manufacturers.

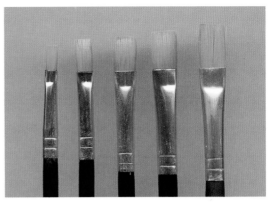

Flats, also called flat shaders, flat wash brushes, or brights, are flat brushes that are squared off. They can either be sized by the measurement of the brush at the top of the ferrule (the metal piece attaching the bristles to the handle) or given a numerical size. So it is possible to have two brushes, one marked as a ⅜" (1cm) flat and one marked as a #10 flat, that are actually the same size. This style of brush is excellent for smooth, even coverage that does not leave a ridge of paint along the sides of the stroke.

Slants, also called slant flats or angular flats, are flat brushes that have the leading brush edge cut at an angle. The slant allows you to carry as much color in the brush as you can with a standard flat shader while also providing a sharp, pointed leading edge for fine line work.

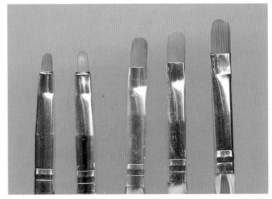

Filberts, also called filbert flats or filbert brights, are flat brushes that have a curved leading edge. This curve creates wonderful, fine feathering work and instant brushstroke petals.

Painting and Coloring Media

Any painting media that can be applied to canvas or paper can be used on your gourd projects, including artist-quality acrylic paints, craft-quality acrylic paints, oil paints, watercolors, colored pencils, watercolor pencils, pastels, and even gel pens. Here is a quick look at the media that you can choose to use on your gourds.

Artist-Quality Colored Pencils
Pictured below are artist-quality, wax-based colored pencils. Colored pencils are available individually, in assorted sets from 12 to 150, and even in pre-selected color ranges for skin tones or shading tones. Student and hobby-quality colored pencils are made with pigment suspended in a chalk base, which makes the pencils hard and opaque. Artist-quality pencils use a wax base, making the coloring semi-transparent, and this allows the pencil color to be applied evenly across the work. Applied in thin layers, artist-quality colored pencils are easy to mix and match to create new color tones.

Artist-Quality Watercolor Pencils
Watercolor pencils are water-soluble. After the layers of colored pencil work are completed, a damp, blotted, soft-bristled brush is used to wet the colors and blend them. Watercolor pencils can also be used over artist-quality colored pencils to add shading and enrich your tonal work. You can use watercolor pencils over a white matte primer to create a transparent wash effect or add shading layers of watercolor pencils over your craft and acrylic paintings to create more gradual, even blends in the design.

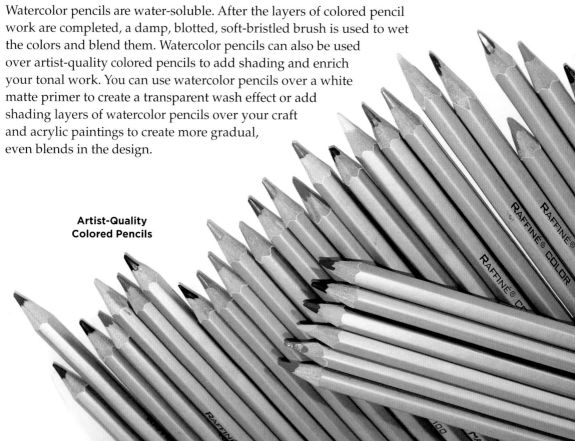

**Artist-Quality
Colored Pencils**

Artist-Quality
Watercolor Pencils

Watercolors

Available in tube or cake form, these paints contain a chemical or mineral
pigment that is suspended in a water-soluble binder such as gum arabic.
Simply add water to create beautiful color washes. Watercolors can
be blended on the gourd surface after application with a damp brush.
Watercolors in gourd art work best over a white matte primer base to keep
your colors crisp and strong. Used directly on your gourd surface, your
painting will take on a muted or sepia-toned look, as the beige-tan coloring
of the gourd shows through the transparency of the watercolors.

Watercolors

Craft and Decorative Acrylic Paints

Available at most hobby and craft stores, this type of painting media is very affordable for any crafter. Craft and decorative acrylics tend to be opaque, giving you solid coverage. Available in a wide variety of hues, shades, and tones, you seldom have to mix your own specific colors. Color names will vary between manufacturers. We will use acrylic craft paints throughout this book.

Artist-Quality Acrylic Paints

Fine, artist-quality acrylics often are transparent or semi-transparent colors, unlike craft-quality paints, which are often opaque, and you may need a primer coat on your gourd (see page 45) before you begin your color application. This type of paint is often sold under the chemical names or chemical combinations used to create that color, such as Cadmium Red Medium or Titanium Dioxide White.

Oil Paints

Artist-quality oil paints contain ground chemicals and minerals suspended in an oil base such as safflower oil or linseed oil. Because of the oil base, these colors dry very slowly, allowing plenty of time for blending and smooth color changes.

Oil Pastels

Oil pastels are ground pigments that are combined with an oil base and then compressed into easy-to-handle sticks. They are available in sets with a full range of colors. You will find them in the drawing aisle of your favorite art supply store.

Gel Pens and Permanent Markers

Gel pens and permanent markers are perfect for creating even, fine lines in a design, especially when you are uncomfortable or inexperienced with a liner brush. If you want to add a personal touch with handwritten names and dates to a project, you can use a gel pen or permanent marker in the exact same manner as you would an ink pen on paper.

General Craft Supplies

There are a lot of assorted, miscellaneous crafting supplies that will come in handy or be indispensable to your gourd-crafting projects, depending on what you choose to do. Here's a quick list of some items you may want to collect and their potential uses.

- Scissors (to cut various supplies)
- Craft knife (to cut openings and holes in gourds)
- #2 to #6 graphite pencil (to make marks on gourds and patterns)
- Tracing or printer paper (to work with patterns)
- 150- and 220-grit sandpaper (to smooth gourds, edges, and modeling compounds)
- Assorted sea sponges (to use for background texturing)
- Clean water (to clean brushes)
- Large bowls (to dip gourds)
- Wax-coated paper plates or Styrofoam plates (to use as paint palettes)
- Wax-coated paper cups (to mix paint)
- Plastic teaspoons (to measure and mix paint)
- Toothbrush (to splatter paint)
- Large, disposable plastic drinking cups (to use as a gourd stand while painting)
- Dishwashing soap (to use with liquid masks)
- Latex gloves (to protect your hands while working)
- Newspaper (to cover and protect your work area)
- Acrylic spray sealer (to finish and protect a project)
- 18- to 24-gauge copper wire (to create hangers and legs)
- Paper rope, raffia cord, ribbon, or paper-covered wire (to use as hanging cords)

A paper plate, a plastic cup, painter's tape, and an old toothbrush set the scene for splattering this gourd.

Specialty Art Supplies

There are several specialized products used throughout this book that warrant a bit more explanation. You will discover that they are very useful for creating beautiful projects and effects.

Acrylic Sculpture Paste

Acrylic sculpture paste is a pre-thickened white paste that can be applied with a brush, palette knife, or sponge. The texture that you create while working with the wet paste will remain after it is thoroughly dry. Sculpture paste is thinned with water, and you can color sculpture paste with acrylic craft paints. In this book, we will be using sculpture paste to create textured designs on top of gourd surfaces as well as to fill in the joint areas where we attach one gourd to another to create a new shape. Once the paste has completely dried, trim the paste areas with a craft knife and sand with 150- to 220-grit sandpaper—unless a highly textured effect is what you're after.

Air-Dry Modeling Clay

Air-dry modeling clay is easily made into new shapes that can be attached to your gourd, and, like sculpture paste, it can be used to fill in the gaps between gourd pieces for constructed projects. Add a few drops of water to your hands if the clay begins to stiffen as you are working. Specially designed modeling clay tools are available for use with the clay, but you can also use your brush handles, Popsicle sticks, and wet brush bristles to shape clay.

Both acrylic sculpture paste and air-dry modeling clay begin to dry as soon as they are exposed to the air. Always clean both the rim and the inside of the jar lid on sculpture paste jars to maintain a tight seal. Store open packages of modeling clay inside zip-top sandwich bags or several folded layers of plastic wrap.

Liquid Mask

Liquid mask is a brush-on frisket—or protective film—that protects the area on which it is applied from coverage of water-based paints. The mask is applied with a brush that has been dipped in water that contains a few drops of dishwashing soap to prevent the mask from adhering to the brush bristles. Once the mask has dried, you simply apply your color, allow the color to dry, and then loosen an edge of the mask to peel it off the project, leaving a clean, unpainted surface behind. Liquid mask is often made of latex.

Archival White Glue

Archival glue is pH-neutral and will not yellow or crack with age. During your gourd crafting, you can use it to glue several gourd pieces together to create new shapes, or to adhere newspaper, burlap, and even hemp string to your gourds. The glue is water-soluble and can be thinned with water to dip and totally saturate cloth or paper that you will be using in your gourd collage work.

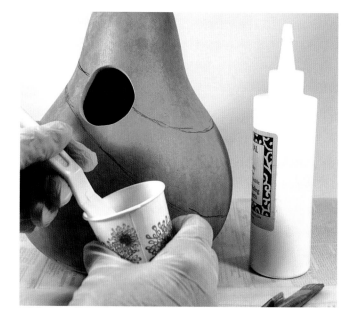

Finely Ground Glitter

Very finely ground glitter can be sprinkled directly onto paint while the color application is still wet. This avoids the extra steps of using glues or spray adhesives, which are typically needed for chunkier glitter. Extra-finely ground glitter is sold online by nail art suppliers.

Reworkable Spray Sealer

There are multiple forms of spray sealers that can be used to give a UV light–resistant and water-resistant finish to your gourd project when it is complete. Sprays are available in an acrylic or polyurethane base as well as in a variety of sheens, any of which will work well for the projects in this book. But as you work your gourd projects, there will be times and steps where a light coat of spray sealer can set the color work that you just completed before you move on to a new step—sealer used during the process rather than as a finishing touch. Reworkable spray sealer (sometimes simply called workable spray sealer) is what you will want in these cases. It creates a thin, fine layer of sealer that has a very light texture, or "tooth," that accepts and holds new layers of color work.

String, Twine, Wire, and Burlap

Just about any craft supply that you use with your other hobbies can be used with your gourd art. In the projects in this book, I have used a variety of ribbons, burlap, art papers, newspaper, feathers, small mesh chicken wire, copper jewelry wire, and other hobby supplies that you may already have on hand. Each project will provide a list of the supplies used.

Low-Tack Painter's Tape

Low-tack masking tape that has a minimal amount of crepe paper texture can be used as a mask on your gourds to prevent color from getting somewhere you don't want it to be. The tape can be used over dried colors that you have already applied as well as on the raw gourd surface. Its uses are similar to that of liquid mask (see page 22), but it is a bit easier to use and less precise.

Spray Adhesive

Spray adhesive can be used to help secure craft supplies like burlap, paper, and ribbon to your gourd until you are ready to hot glue or archival glue the item permanently in place. Read the instructions on your spray can to achieve temporary or permanent adhesion, depending on your needs.

Gourd Preparation

Gourd Shapes and Sizes

Gourds come in a wide variety of shapes and sizes. Shown in the photo below are a large kettle gourd, a medium canteen gourd, a small gooseneck gourd, and two small egg gourds. Gourds are first classified by the name of their general shape (such as kettle, canteen, gooseneck, and egg), then by their size; finally, a note may be added as to whether a gourd is thick-walled, blemished, or has some coloration variations on the outer shell. Gourds are measured in height, diameter, and circumference. A kettle gourd might be noted as being 9" (23cm) high, 6" (15cm) in diameter, and 19" (48cm) in circumference—where the diameter and circumference are always around the widest part of the gourd.

Because of the nature of the gourd art techniques taught in this book, while the size and shape that I use will be given in each supply list, no specific size or shape of gourd is required. Where I may use a canteen gourd, you might choose a large apple gourd, and where I may use a medium egg gourd, you can easily substitute a small gooseneck gourd.

No gourd is absolutely perfect. Working with the peculiarities of any gourd is part of the fun of gourd art. With the addition of acrylic sculpture paste to your craft kit (see page 21), many of the projects in this book can be perfect for that stash of blemished, scarred, and distorted gourds that you have been setting aside over the years.

Avoiding Mold and Dust–Stay Healthy!

Any gourd, whether it is fresh out of the barn or purchased through the mail, will require some preparation before you begin a project.

Gourds grow with a natural waxy covering that protects the gourd shell and seeds from water during the winter months. As the gourd dries, this wax begins to develop a layer of mold that eats it, exposing the wood-like shell to the elements. The shell can now crack, break, rot, and open, releasing the seeds in the spring. The inside of your gourd can also contain mold and dust.

Any type of mold or fine dust can be hazardous if inhaled, so wear a dust mask while you are cleaning your gourds. Latex gloves can also be used to avoid coming in direct contact with the natural dust and mold any gourd has. Work your cleaning and sanding steps in a well-ventilated room.

Preparing a Gourd

Supplies

- Dust mask
- Latex gloves
- Dishwashing soap
- Steel wool soap pad
- Paper towels
- #2 to #6 graphite pencil
- Assorted books
- Utility knife or bench knife
- Long-handled teaspoon or palette knife
- Terry cloth towel

1 **Wash the gourd.** Begin any gourd project by taking the gourd to the sink and giving the outer surface a good, hard scrubbing using warm water, dishwashing soap, and a steel wool pad. This removes any remaining mold spores, garden dirt, and dust. After a good rinse in clean water, let the gourd dry on a few sheets of paper towel.

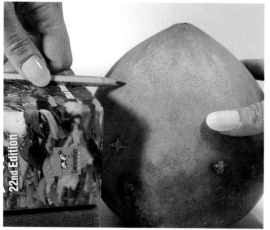

2 **Create a straight cutting line.** For tall gourds, rest a pencil on a stack of books that measures the height of where you want your top cut for a pot or vase. Turn the gourd, keeping the gourd wall against the pencil, to create a level pencil cutting line.

3 **Score along the guideline.** Use a sturdy utility knife or bench knife to score a cut along the pencil guideline. Use short, shallow strokes to slowly deepen the cutting line. Do not puncture the gourd just yet.

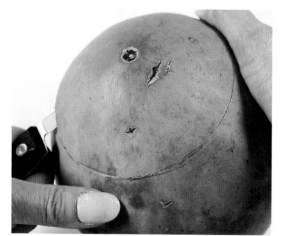

4 **Pierce the guideline.** After thoroughly scoring the guideline, cut until the knife goes completely through the shell wall. Cut all the way around the guidelines. Do not pry or force the cut section to free itself from the gourd. On some thin-shelled gourds, this can crack the side of the gourd.

5 **Remove the insides.** Remove the seedpods and set the cut section aside for use in construction projects. The seeds can be saved and planted in your garden next spring.

6 **Scrape out the insides.** Use a long-handled teaspoon or sturdy palette knife to loosen any remaining seedpod and pod fibers inside the gourd. Remove all of the loose seeds and debris.

7 **Soak the inside of the gourd.** Completely fill the inside of the gourd with warm water and allow it to sit for a few moments. This dampens the dust, dirt, and mold spores so that they cannot become airborne. I often fill and rinse the inside of my gourds several times during the cleaning process, as it is an easy way to clear the gourd of loosened fibers.

8 **Continue to clean.** Use a long-handled teaspoon or sturdy palette knife to scrape the damp inside walls. Remove all the fibers until you have reached the wood-like inner shell.

9 **Finish.** Give the gourd a second scrubbing with soap and warm water. Set it upside down on a towel and allow it to dry completely before moving on to the surface preparation steps (see page 31).

Creating a Straight Cutting Line on Irregularly Shaped Gourds

Some gourds have extremely rounded or irregular bottoms, and some tilt or twist to one side, making it hard to establish a level cutting line using a pencil on a stack of books or using a ruler. For these oddly shaped gourds, you can use water to create a perfectly level line for cutting. (Note: The water in these photos has been tinted red as a visual aid to show the concept.)

1 **Mark the gourd.** Fill a deep bowl two-thirds full of water. Hold the gourd at the top and determine at what angle you want the gourd to hang—basically, where you want the cutting line to fall. Make a pencil mark or marks as desired as a guide to where you want the cutting line. In this example, I drew four lines down the sides of the gourd as indicators.

2 **Dip the gourd.** Keeping the hanging angle steady, slowly lower the gourd into the water bowl until the water touches the pencil mark(s). Stop and hold the gourd in the water for a few moments so that the lower section becomes thoroughly dampened.

3 **Mark the cutting line.** Lift the gourd out of the water. The gourd will have a clear, level water line around its circumference. Use a pencil to mark along this line; this will become your cutting line. Most medium gourds can be dipped in your kitchen sink. For larger gourds, use a three-gallon (eleven-liter) bucket or even your bathtub.

Surface Preparation

Before you actually proceed with the artistic aspects of any gourd project, you will need to pre-treat the gourd surface in a variety of ways to create a solid base for crafting. Depending on the state of your gourd, you may not need to do all of these tasks, but you will probably need to do many of them most of the time. Usually the surface preparation should take place after all gourd cleaning (inside and outside) is completed. Before beginning any project, think about the logical order to follow for preparing, cleaning, and crafting.

Supplies

- 220-grit sandpaper
- Craft knife
- Ox-hair brush
- Water
- Acrylic sculpture paste
- Paper plate or sheet of tinfoil
- Palette knife
- ½" (1cm) eye screw (optional)

1 Sand. Sand any blemishes, scars, and small holes with 220-grit sandpaper.

2 Cut open the holes. Use a craft knife to open up small holes, creating cone-shaped walls that will not trap air when sculpture paste is added.

3 Remove dust. Dampen a stiff-bristled ox-hair brush with water. Scrub each area that you have worked with the brush to remove the fine dust left from the sanding.

4 Allow to dry. Let the gourd dry until it has lost its glossy look but is still damp. A slightly damp surface will allow the sculpture paste to create a tighter bond to the gourd walls.

5 Fill the holes. Place a small amount of sculpture paste on a paper plate or sheet of tinfoil. Pick up some paste on the tip of a palette knife and fill each of the holes.

6 Finish the holes. Smooth the sculpture paste with a damp finger. Allow the paste to dry. Small, shallow areas can dry quite quickly, within fifteen minutes. Large areas that need filling may require several layers of sculpture paste, slowly building up the paste to the surface level of the gourd. Allow each layer to dry for at least an hour before adding the next application.

7 Sand. Lightly sand the dry sculpture paste patches with 220-grit sandpaper to remove any ridges and to smooth the area to conform to the surface of the gourd.

8 Add finishing touches. If you are planning to hang your gourd, see page 42 for instructions on adding an eye screw.

Construction Skills

Thanks to glues, air-dry modeling clay, and acrylic sculpture paste, you are in no way limited to the shape of a single gourd for your gourd projects. You can attach and shape multiple gourds however you like. Pieces from previously cut gourds and small gourds can be added to your main gourd bowl to create new forms. Read on for detailed instructions for creating a standing bird (the Newspaper Collage Bird, page 158), complete with head, beak, tail, and legs. You can apply the skills learned here to any gourd construction project.

Supplies

- 11" (28cm) high, 7" (18cm) diameter, 20" (51cm) circumference kettle or canteen gourd, cut as a bowl
- 1 small round egg gourd
- 1 small oval egg gourd
- #2 to #6 graphite pencil
- Utility knife or bench knife
- 18-gauge or thinner copper wire
- 20-gauge copper wire
- Flush cutters
- Straight-nosed pliers
- Ruler
- Permanent marker
- Hot glue gun and glue
- Superglue
- Air-dry modeling clay
- Modeling clay tools
- Acrylic sculpture paste
- Palette knife
- 220-grit sandpaper

Fitting the Head and Tail

1 **Mark the head.** Select two small egg gourds—one round and one oval—to become the head and tail of the bird. Holding the round egg gourd against the top edge of the large cut kettle gourd, mark the cutting lines on the egg gourd with a pencil. For this bird, I allowed about one-third of the egg gourd to sit above the cut edge of the larger gourd. This created a triangular cutting line for my project.

2 **Prepare the head.** Follow the procedure (see page 27) for preparing the egg gourd, including washing, cutting, and cleaning the inside.

3 **Check the fit.** Place the cut egg gourd into position against the larger gourd for a dry-fit check. Re-cut along the guidelines as necessary until the egg gourd sits tightly against the larger gourd. It does not need to be a perfectly snug fit; we will be using either sculpture paste or modeling clay to fill in the small gaps.

4 **Mark the tail.** Position the oval egg gourd on the opposite side of the round egg gourd head. Rough in pencil guidelines where this small gourd will attach to the larger gourd. Cut along the guidelines and clean the inside of the egg gourd.

5 **Mark the tail position.** Holding the oval egg gourd in position against the larger gourd, mark along the center of the egg gourd where you want the tail section to stop.

6 **Check the fit.** Cut along the tail guideline. This will leave the oval egg gourd in two pieces of almost equal size. Dry fit and adjust the tail section to a snug fit against the larger gourd. Then set the head and tail pieces aside: they will be attached to the main gourd after the copper wire legs are created and installed. You are now ready to trim the cut edges using a utility knife or bench knife and to sand all the surfaces—inside and out—using 150- to 220-grit sandpaper. (See page 52, in Wind Chime Construction, for further instructions on sanding.)

Creating Copper Wire Legs

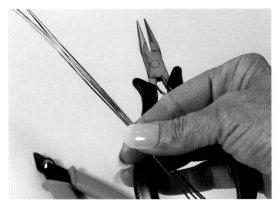

7 **Cut the wire.** With flush cutters, cut four lengths of 18-gauge copper wire that are each 14" (36cm) long. Each leg will be made from two wires.

8 **Fold the wire.** Measure 7" (18cm) from one end to find the center point of each wire. Mark this point with a permanent marker. Grip two of the wires together at the marked point in a pair of straight-nosed pliers and fold the wires over the pliers to create a tight U-bend.

9 **Wrap the wire.** Measure two 30" (76cm) to 36" (92cm) lengths of 20-gauge copper wire, one for each leg. Hold one end of a 20-gauge wire extending ¾" (2cm) out from the U-bend loop of one pair of leg wires. Wrap the 20-gauge wire in a tight cluster of ten coils around all four strands of the leg wires. Continue wrapping the wire down along the leg wires for about 4" (10cm) in a loose coil pattern. Create a tight cluster wrap of 10 coils, overlapping the wires as you wrap in one small spot. Repeat this process for the other leg.

10 **Finish the legs.** The U-bend loop end of the copper legs will go inside the gourd. The four unwrapped ends will become the toes of the bird. Clip the four end wires flush to each other on each leg, removing as little wire as possible. You can trim these toes again if needed after the legs are set into position.

Attaching the Legs

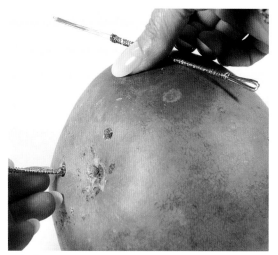

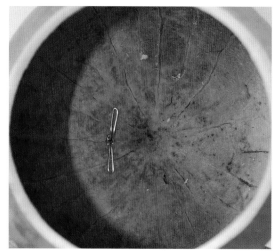

11 **Cut leg holes.** Using a utility knife, mark and cut two holes in the bottom of the larger gourd that are just slightly larger than the diameter of the legs.

12 **Insert the legs.** Slide the U-bend loop end of one leg into one of the holes. Fold the two loops open to lock the leg tightly against the base of the gourd. Repeat with the other leg.

Creative Legs

Your copper legs are a great place to be creative. When I worked the construction steps for the Netting Bird (page 112), I gripped the ends of the toe wires in round-nosed pliers and rolled a small loop. This added a little extra stability as well as creating a small accent on the feet. I also added knees to the bird by wrapping a length of 20-gauge wire around the legs about 1″ (2.5cm) below the joining point with the gourd.

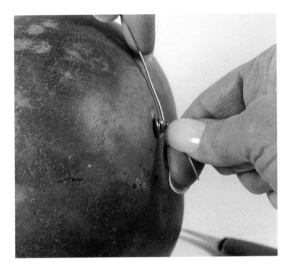

13 **Add more wire wrapping.** With one 12" (30.5cm) to 14" (35.5cm) length of 20-gauge copper wire for each leg, wrap a tight cluster of 10 to 12 coils around the base of each leg where it enters the bottom of the gourd.

14 **Glue the legs.** Lay a thick layer of hot glue over the loops inside the gourd to secure the legs and prevent them from moving or rotating. You can also cut and shape a small section of an egg gourd to place over the hot glue area inside the gourd. This will cover up the copper wire and glue area, leaving the inside with a clean, finished look.

15 **Fold the toes.** Allow the hot glue to cool and set completely, then fold and bend the four unwrapped wire lengths at the end of each leg into a chicken foot position: three toes pointing forward and one toe pointing back.

Gluing the Pieces Together

16 **Cut the beak.** From the remaining oval gourd scrap, cut two small triangular pieces that will become the upper and lower bird beaks. I made my upper beak slightly larger than my lower so that the lower piece would sit inside the top piece.

17 **Glue the pieces together.** Using hot glue along the cut edge of the egg gourd head, set the head into place on the larger gourd. Use the glue sparingly, as this is just to hold the gourd in place until sculpture paste or modeling clay is applied. Attach the tail and two beak sections in the same way.

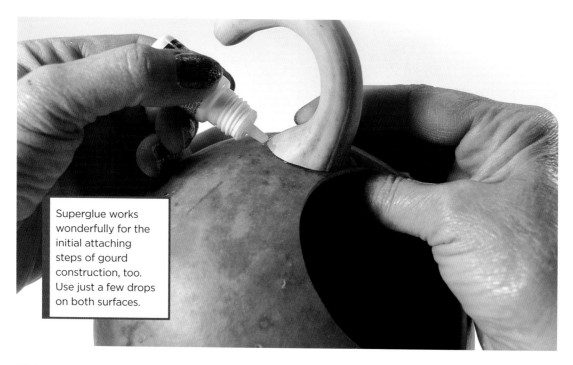

Superglue works wonderfully for the initial attaching steps of gourd construction, too. Use just a few drops on both surfaces.

Sculpting the Shape

18 **Get ready to sculpt.** With the general shape created and set into place using hot glue or superglue, it's time to fill and shape the joint areas between the large gourd and smaller pieces. You can use either air-dry modeling clay or sculpture paste for the following steps. Here, I used modeling clay. Instructions for using sculpture paste are shown with the Dab Pitcher project (page 86).

19 **Prepare the clay.** Remove a small piece of modeling clay from the package. Reseal the package immediately to prevent the nonworking portion from drying out. Roll the small piece of clay in your hands to create a long, wormlike shape. If the clay feels dry or cracks during the rolling process, add a few drops of water to your hands to refresh the clay.

20 **Apply the clay.** Push the log of clay into the joint area between the head and body of the bird.

21 **Smooth the clay.** Use your fingers and a few drops of water to smooth and shape the clay to create an even, gentle curve between the two pieces.

22 **Add clay to all the joints.** Use modeling clay to transition the joints for the beak pieces and tail of the bird. Set the piece aside for 24 hours to allow the clay to dry completely.

Sanding the Finished Construction

23 **Sand.** Once the piece is completely dry, you can use 220-grit sandpaper to smooth out any small ridges left from the shaping steps. The bird is ready to be painted!

Creating the Blown Bird Construction

This fun copper wire–legged bird was created using
five different gourds with four different densities and
surface textures. Because of time constraints, I allowed
the sculpture paste used in the joints to become far
too hard to sand to a smooth, even surface. When I
was finally able to return to this project, I had to ask
myself what I wanted to do. Should I abandon the
project because of its obvious physical problems, or
move ahead using those problems to my advantage?
Of course I chose to move ahead, and this rough and
crude gourd construction became my favorite gourd
project. Because I couldn't get rid of the physical
problems—the rough and crude surface—I decided
to use the irregularities to my advantage, as you will
discover as you work the Blown Bird project (page 106).

Special Skills

In this section, we will review some special skills that might come in handy as you work on your gourd projects.

Preparing a Birdhouse

Gourds make wonderful birdhouses. They provide a large, well-protected cavity for your favorite backyard birds to nest in while giving you lots of creative space. There are a few simple steps that you can take to make any birdhouse a better, long-term nesting space.

Every birdhouse needs several small holes in the top neck area or hanging area of the gourd to provide air movement and ventilation. Use a utility knife or bench knife to make three to four ¼" (0.5cm) holes about ½" (1cm) to 1" (2.5cm) from the stem point of the gourd.

Pre-drill a small ⅛" (0.3cm) hole in the stem area of the gourd in which to set a large eye screw. You can reinforce the screw area, giving it extra strength, by working a small amount of sculpture paste around the base of the screw.

Bird Watcher's Digest

For more information about bird nesting habits to inform your birdhouse crafting, check out the following website:
https://www.birdwatchersdigest .com/bwdsite/learn/top10/ nestingbirds.php

Adding a Trapdoor

Your favorite backyard birds may raise up to three broods each year. For each new brood, they will need a clean, empty nesting space. If you want to easily tend to a gourd birdhouse and encourage a nesting pair to stay in the nest, you should add a trapdoor, which is an easy method of cleaning the gourd between laying sessions. This trapdoor at the bottom of the birdhouse does double duty as the opening you use to initially clean out the inside of the gourd.

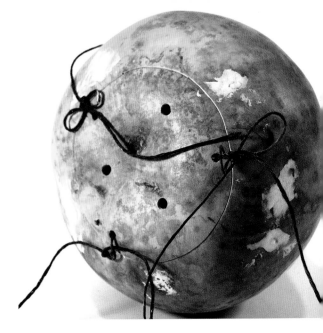

Supplies

- Compass
- Pencil
- Craft knife
- 220-grit sandpaper
- Waxed linen cord
- Darning or needlepoint dull-point needle
- Scissors

1 Draw the door. Using a compass and pencil, draw a large 3" (7.5cm) to 4" (10cm) circle on the bottom of the gourd.

2 Mark cord holes. Mark three equidistant points around the inside edges of the pencil circle to position the holes for a waxed linen cord that will tie the trapdoor to the main body of the gourd. Mark three points around the outside edges of the pencil circle that are right next to the first three points.

3 Mark drainage holes. Mark three points centrally inside the circle for drainage holes.

4 Cut out the door. Using a craft knife, cut out the circle.

5 Clean. While the bottom is open, finish any necessary cleaning steps inside the gourd.

6 Bore the holes. Use the point of the craft knife to bore the nine holes that you have marked. You can make all of these holes fairly large, as the thread holes can also act as drainage holes.

7 Sand. Lightly sand the circle and the bottom cut edges.

8 Temporarily tie the door closed. To temporarily hold the trapdoor in place during the painting steps, thread waxed linen cord on a dull-pointed needle through the holes and tie closed.

9 Replace the door ties. After the painting is complete, you can re-tie this trapdoor in place with a clean waxed linen cord.

10 Use, clean, and replace. After each nesting session is complete, you can cut the thread, clean the gourd, and re-string the trapdoor in preparation for the next brood.

Tying a Surgeon's Knot

In my experience, simple square knots can seldom be tightened sufficiently to secure a cord, nor do they remain tightly tied over time. The surgeon's knot adds one extra twist in each loop of a square knot, making it extremely secure and tight.

1 Thread the cord through the hole. Cross the two threads to create a loop. Thread one end of the cord through that loop to make the first part or twist of a square knot.

2 Then thread the same cord end through the loop one more time. This makes two twists through the loop.

> For cords or threads that will be worked on indoor decorative gourds, I use bailing twine, burlap twine, burlap braided cord, and even colored cotton cords. For outdoor projects, however, I prefer to use nylon cords or waxed linen cords, as both are water-repellent and will therefore hold up better to the elements.

3 Pull tight.

4 Repeat the double twists (steps 1 and 2) for the second part of the knot. Pull tight. That one extra looping twist holds the first portion of the knot secure while you work the second twist.

Working with Primers

A primer is an acrylic base coat that is applied over a raw surface before the individual colors are painted. Primer blocks out the uneven, blotchy surface coloring that some gourds have naturally, creating a matte surface that is more controllable than the raw gourd during color application, and allowing the paints to take on a bright, clean appearance.

Water-based, matte acrylic primers are available in colors (such as white, black, gray, and medium beige), or you can add small amounts of craft paint to them to tint the primer coat to the desired shade. Pre-mixed primers often have little or no shine, which allows the paint to adhere well. However, most pre-mixed primers are pure white and have a gritty finish. If you are using a pre-mixed primer, thin it on a palette with 2 parts primer to 1 part water.

You can also create your own primer using the paints you have on hand, which is what I prefer to do. I usually thin my primer with several drops of water added to a quarter-sized puddle of primer on the palette. The extra water in the mix slows the drying rate of the paint to give you extra time to smooth out each brushful of color.

The colors you will be using on your project determine what color of primer you should use. Use white primer when you

White primer like this one will make colors painted over it very vivid and pure.

want bright and vivid coloring or when you want to work pastel shades. If an area will be red, orange, purple, bright green, or bright blue, you can use a pale gray primer. Beige and mid-tone gray primers are excellent for your paintings that are predominantly in the yellow through red hues. Mustard yellow, tan, and medium brown primers work well for yellows, medium and dull greens, orange, rust, teal, and skin tones. Black primers make dramatic backgrounds for oil pastel and colored pencil work, allowing the colors to really pop against the dark surface.

For some projects, you may want a primer coat made up of several blended colors. For example, you can place a small amount of golden yellow, tan, and medium brown on your palette. As you apply the primer coat, you can randomly pick up a little color from each color puddle. The colors will blend as you brush them onto the gourd, giving the primer a mottled effect. Using a varied, blended primer adds to the mottled, textured appearance of the color coats. If your final color application will be an uneven, blended coloring, try using a blended primer as your base coat.

You may want to prime the inside of a gourd, too, if you are planning on painting it.

CHAPTER 2

Smooth Projects

NOW THAT YOU KNOW all about how to prepare gourds and assemble them into your desired shapes, it's time for the painting and crafting to begin! In this chapter, we will look at a variety of interesting ways to apply paint to your gourd projects to make interesting and stunning effects. We will blow, dab, drip, splatter, and more. By the time you've tried each of the projects in this chapter, you'll have an entire repertoire of cool paint techniques you can apply to any project.

Throughout the projects in this book, always wash, clean, and cut all gourds following the general preparation instructions before proceeding with the crafting steps. Follow all necessary steps to clean out the insides, protect yourself from dust and mold, and sand edges carefully.

Wind Chime Construction

I love to work a practice piece, where I can play, experiment, and make mistakes without damaging my main project gourds. Small gourds, measuring 3" (7.5cm) to 4" (10cm) in diameter, not only work well as practice gourds, but they can also become delightful little wind chimes for your back porch. Here, we will look at the general steps for creating a gourd wind chime that can then be used in upcoming projects.

Supplies

- 4" (10cm) high, 4" (10cm) diameter, 12" (30.5cm) circumference kettle gourd
- Utility knife or bench knife
- Medium-sized paper drinking cup
- #2 to #6 graphite pencil
- Water-based wood glue
- Long-handled teaspoon
- Palette knife
- Large plastic zip-top bag
- 150- and 220-grit sandpaper
- Acrylic craft paint primer
- Acrylic craft paint
- 18-gauge copper wire
- Straight-nosed pliers
- Round-nosed pliers
- Flush cutters
- Small beads, tassels, and gourd pieces for trim

Cutting and Preparing the Gourd

1 Wash the gourd. Read and follow the general preparation steps for washing the gourd (see page 27) before you begin the cutting steps.

2 Set up the cutting line. To determine the cutting line for the opening at the bottom of the wind chime gourd, set the gourd in a paper drinking cup. Position the gourd in the cup so that it has an upright stance.

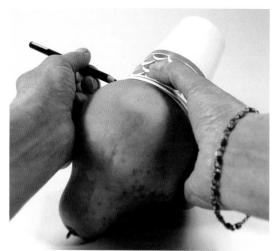

3 Draw the cutting line. Use a #2 to #6 pencil, pulling it along the top edge of the paper cup, to mark the cutting line.

4 Check the cutting line. You can see in this photo that your cutting line is often not perfectly centered on the blossom end of the gourd because of the natural irregularities in the shape of any gourd.

5 **Cut the gourd.** Use a very sharp bench knife or craft knife to cut thin-walled gourds. A sharp knife avoids the need to use extra pressure, which can crack the gourd walls.

When cutting extremely thin-walled gourds, like egg gourds, follow these steps to help prevent cracking:

- Lay a narrow bead of water-based wood glue just above the cutting line of the section that you will not be using for your project.
- Let the glue dry for an hour to set up, and then lay a second beading of glue over the first.
- Let the glue dry overnight. The glue adds a little strength reinforcement against the pressure of the knife cut and helps keep thin-walled gourds from cracking.

6 **Set aside the cut section.** Save the cut bottom section of the gourd to use as part of the clapper decoration.

7 **Clean the inside.** Follow the general directions for cleaning the inside of the gourd (see pages 28–29). Empty the gourd of any seeds and seedpod fibers. Small gourds like this one can easily be emptied into a large plastic bag to reduce the dust and debris at your worktable.

8 **Soak and scrape the inside.** Soak the inside of the gourd in water, allowing the seeds, debris, and fibers to become thoroughly wet. Scrap the inside using a long-handled teaspoon or palette knife. The tool shown in the photo is a chemist's spatula, which is very rigid but thin and makes cleaning the inside of your gourd fast and easy.

9 **Clean up the edges.** Trim along the cut edge with a utility knife or bench knife to level the edges and to remove any rough areas along the inside of the gourd.

10 **Sand the gourd.** Sand the outside surface of the gourd using 220-grit sandpaper. Be sure to sand along the cut edges.

11 **Finish the preparation.** Sand the inside of the gourd first with 150-grit sandpaper, then with 220-grit sandpaper. Rinse the gourd, inside and out, with clean water to remove the dust.

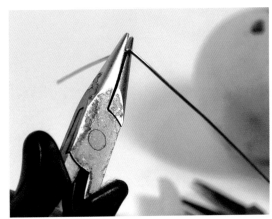

For an absolutely even, perfectly cut edge:
- Tape a full, 9″ x 12″ (23 x 30.5cm) sheet of 150-grit sandpaper, face up, to a 12″ x 12″ x ¼″ (30.5 x 30.5 x 0.5cm) piece of plywood.
- Clamp the sandpaper-covered plywood board to your worktable to stabilize it.
- Turn the gourd upside down onto the sandpaper, putting the cut edge in contact with the sandpaper.
- You can now rub the gourd in circular motions over the sandpaper and sand the edge to a perfectly flat finish.

12 **Apply primer.** After the gourd has dried completely, apply one to two coats of acrylic primer to the inside. Any color of acrylic craft paint can be used inside of a gourd wind chime. Apply one to two coats to achieve full coverage.

Creating a Copper Wire Hanger

1 **Cut a hanging hole.** With a bench knife, cut a small hole, about ⅛″ (0.3cm) wide, in the center top (the stem area) of the gourd wind chime.

2 **Bend the wire.** Cut an 8″ (20cm) length of 18-gauge copper wire. Grip the wire in straight-nosed pliers 2″ (5cm) from one end. Bend the wire over the edge of the pliers into a right angle.

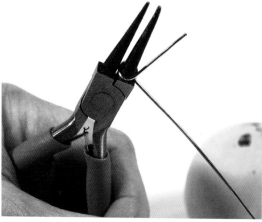

3 **Create a loop.** Move the bent wire into a pair of round-nosed pliers, placing the right angle against one side of the round tips. Roll the short end of the wire around the round-nosed pliers' side to create a small loop.

4 **Wrap the wire.** Move the wire back into the straight-nosed pliers, gripping the loop inside of the pliers. With your thumb, roll the excess wire left on the short end of the loop around the base of the long end of the wire for three turns. Use flush cutters to trim off any remaining wire left from the wrapping. You have now made a wrapped straight loop, a common wire shape in wire-wrapped jewelry making.

5 **Insert the wire.** Slide the wire inside the gourd and up through the hole at the top so that the wrapped straight loop is on the inside of the wind chime.

6 **Bend the top wire.** With the wrapped straight loop snug against the inside top of the gourd, you will make a new wrapped straight loop on the outside piece of wire. Begin by gripping the wire in straight-nosed pliers where the wire comes out of the gourd and making a right-angle bend.

7 **Create the top wrapped loop.** Create the loop by gripping the wire in the round-nosed pliers just above the right angle bend. Return to the straight-nosed pliers to grip the loop as you wrap the remaining wire around the base of the loop three to four times. Trim off any excess wire using flush cutters. Be careful not to add too many turns around the base wire during this step—forcing an extra wrap can cause the wire link to become so tight against the gourd that it cracks the gourd.

8 **Create a chain.** You can create copper wire chains by working one wrapped straight loop linked to another.

There are many free online tutorials, projects, and videos that can teach you how to create your own bent-wire and wire-wrapped jewelry pieces that can be used to accent your gourd art.

9 **Create a hook.** Small hooks can be worked at the end of the chain to catch the wrapped loop on the inside of the gourd. Work a wrapped straight loop at the top loop of the chain. Grip the remaining wire in round-nosed pliers about ¼" (0.5cm) away from the wrapped loop. Bend the wire over the round-nosed pliers' side to create a U-bend. Clip the excess wire from the open side of the bend to finish the hook.

10 **Add decoration.** Small beads, tassels, and even cut and sanded gourd pieces can be added to a hooked chain to become the clapper for the wind chime.

11 **Attach the chain.** The hook end of this chain latches onto the inside wrapped straight loop to create a free-swinging clapper.

Creating a Modeling Clay Clapper

All three of the wind chime projects in this book (pages 58, 68, and 80) use a large circular clay accent in their clapper decoration. Here is how to make it.

1 Prepare the clay. Begin with a small piece of air-dry modeling clay about the size of a golf ball. Work the clay in your hands to soften it.

2 Flatten the clay. Place the clay ball on a sheet of wax paper and, with the palm of your hand, flatten it to about ¼" (0.5cm) thick. With a rolling pin, continue flattening the ball slightly until it has a smooth, uniform thickness.

3 Make sure the clay remains smooth. Do not over-press the clay, as this can cause cracking along the edges. If the clay begins to dry too quickly, just place a few drops of water on your hand and lightly pat your hand on the clay. This will transfer a small amount of water at a time.

4 Cut the clapper shape. With a cookie cutter, cut out the desired clapper shape. Use a plastic straw to cut a hole in the top and bottom of the circle to allow for adding copper wire.

5 Allow to dry. Loosely place a second sheet of wax paper on top of the clay shape to allow it to dry slowly. Every few hours, gently lift and turn the clay shape over to let both sides dry evenly. Allow the clay to dry completely; it will take about 24 hours.

6 Make multiple clappers. While you have the clay, rolling pin, and cookie cutter out, make several clay clappers. You will always have a dry clapper ready to go when you make another wind chime.

Dip Wind Chime

With this charming project, you'll learn how to create a blended, sea-sponged background and how to accent that background by repeatedly dipping the gourd in water-thinned color. Liquid mask is used to protect the flower design on this wind chime during the dipping steps, leaving the pattern area clean of background color and ready to be painted.

Supplies

- 4" (10cm) high, 4" (10cm) diameter, 12" (30.5cm) circumference kettle gourd
- Sea sponge
- Wax-coated paper plates
- Tracing or printer paper
- Painter's tape
- Scissors or craft knife
- Pen
- #2 to #6 graphite pencil
- Liquid mask
- Dishwashing soap
- Clean water
- Large bowl for dipping
- Plastic teaspoons
- Latex gloves
- Large, disposable plastic drinking cup
- Toothbrush
- Newspaper (to cover work area)
- Acrylic spray sealer
- #4 red sable round brush

- #6 red sable round brush
- #1 or #2 red sable liner brush
- Acrylic craft paint:
  - Titanium white
  - Medium lavender
  - Pale blue
  - Medium turquoise
  - Dark turquoise
  - Metallic gold
  - Medium bright yellow
  - Medium green
  - Dark pink
  - Pale yellow cream
  - Magenta pink
  - Black
- 18-gauge copper wire
- Flush cutters
- Straight-nosed pliers
- Round-nosed pliers
- Assorted beads, tassels/ribbons, and air-dry modeling clay for the clapper decoration

Applying the Sponge Base Coat

1 **Prepare the gourd.** Clean, cut, and sand a small kettle gourd into a wind chime base. Place a small amount of medium lavender and titanium white paint on the palette.

2 **Prepare the sponge.** Dampen a sea sponge with clean water. Tightly squeeze the sponge to remove any excess water; you want it just slightly damp. Choose a well-textured area of the sponge. Tap that area into the puddle of white paint, then on the palette several times to saturate the sponge fibers with white paint. Tap half of the same area into the lavender puddle, then tap it several times on the palette again. This double-loads the sponge and blends the two colors in the sponge fibers.

3 **Apply lavender.** With the lavender side of the sponge against the cut opening of the wind chime, tap the sponge all around the lower edge of the gourd.

4 **Apply white.** Wash the sponge well and squeeze out any excess water. Load the sponge with just titanium white and tap the color on the unpainted area of the gourd. Allow to dry. Repeat these steps with a second coat if necessary.

Tracing and Masking the Pattern

5 **Apply the pattern.** Make a copy of the small flower pattern (page 66) on printer paper. Cut around the pattern, leaving a ¼" (0.5cm) margin. Rub the back of the paper with a soft graphite pencil. Cut slices in the paper between the petals and leaves to allow the paper to fold onto the gourd as you trace the design. With the pencil rubbing against the gourd, use several pieces of painter's tape to hold the pattern in place. Trace the design with a pen.

6 **Check the transfer.** Make sure the pattern lines have all transferred successfully. The finished tracing will be a pale to medium gray that can easily be erased without damaging the sponged background.

7 **Apply the mask.** Following the directions on the product, apply one coat of liquid mask to the entire pattern area. Allow to dry until the masked area has lost its wet, milky appearance.

A soft-bristled brush, such as a synthetic or red sable, works best for applying liquid mask. Always remember to add a few drops of dishwashing soap to the water to prevent the mask from adhering to the brush bristles.

Dipping and Splattering

8 **Mix pale blue paint.** Choose a bowl large enough to dip at least half of the gourd. Fill it two-thirds full of clean water. Add three to four teaspoons of pale blue paint to the water and stir well. This creates a very thin mix.

9 **Dip the gourd.** Wearing latex gloves, grip the wind chime by the bottom opening and dip the gourd into the paint and water mix, tilting the gourd to one side. Hold the gourd still for just a few moments to let the paint mix create a straight line along the gourd. Slowly remove the gourd from the paint and water mix, holding it over the bowl to allow the gourd to drip. When the dripping stops, set the gourd on your workspace.

10 **Darken the paint.** Add two to three teaspoons of medium turquoise paint to the paint and water mix, and stir well.

11 **Dip the gourd.** Turn the gourd to a new angle, then dip it into the new color mix. This will create a new straight line of color across the gourd. Hold the gourd over the bowl until the dripping stops.

12 **Create a marbled mix.** Add two to three teaspoons of dark turquoise to the color and paint mix. Stir lightly in a swirling motion, but do not over-mix. The new color will partially mix, leaving obvious color lines on the surface of the paint water.

13 **Dip the gourd.** Turn the gourd again and dip it into the new color mixture. Slowly remove the gourd from the color and paint mix, allowing the excess color to drip back into the bowl. Turn the gourd again to a new area and dip it again, using the same color and water mix.

14 **Splatter the gourd.** Place a teaspoon of metallic gold acrylic paint onto a clean area of the palette. Dampen an old toothbrush in clean water. Tap the brush onto a folded paper towel to remove any excess water. Load the bristles of the brush in the gold paint. Holding the brush with the bristles facing up, pull your thumb across the bristles, working from the tip of the brush nearest the gourd back toward your hand. This will flip or spring the bristles of the toothbrush, causing the paint to splatter across the gourd. Splatter the entire gourd, turning the gourd as you work. For very fine splatter dots, do not thin the paint. Use it at the jar or bottle consistency. For large dots, add a few drops of water to the paint puddle on the palette: thinner paint makes larger drops.

Painting the Design

15 **Remove the mask.** Set the gourd upside down on an inverted tall plastic cup to dry thoroughly for about one hour. When it is dry, gently rub your finger from a colored background area into the liquid mask area to make the mask edge roll away from the gourd. Grip the small roll in your fingers and peel the remaining mask from the gourd.

16 **Check the final result.** The finished dipped background will have varying color lines from each color dip, swirls from the partially mixed dip, and even lovely drips from the excess color application. The splattering adds a little overall sparkle to the changing color background.

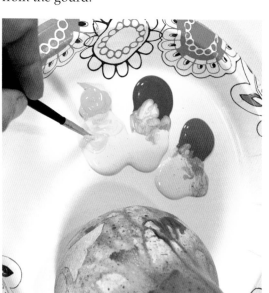

17 **Paint the petals.** Place a small amount of medium bright yellow, medium green, dark pink, and pale yellow cream paint onto the palette. With a #4 to #6 round brush, lightly fill one petal of the flower with dark pink. Add a small amount of pale yellow cream to the pink to create a medium pink and paint two more petals with this. Add a little more pale yellow cream to the pink mix for the last flower petal.

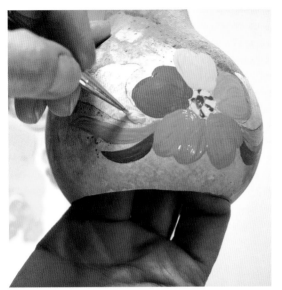

18 **Paint the leaves and center.** Paint the bottom leaf of the design with medium green. Add a small amount of pale yellow cream to the green for the middle leaf. Add more pale yellow cream to the green mix for the last, top leaf. At this stage, also paint the center of the flower with medium green and pale yellow cream.

19 **Prepare the petal center paint.** Place a small amount of magenta pink onto the palette. Thin some of the magenta with a damp #6 round brush.

20 **Paint the petal centers.** Load the brush with the thinned magenta and lay the brush in the lower two-thirds of each petal to create a thumbprint effect. This is just a touch, push, and lift stroke.

21 **Paint the outlines.** With a #1 or #2 liner brush and black paint, outline the traced pattern lines around the entire flower. Add a few thin lines inside each petal, working the stroke from the center of the flower out toward the edge.

22 **Add dots.** Using the brush handle dipped in black paint, make small dots at the end of each of the fine black lines.

Small flower pattern (copy at 200%)

Finishing

23 **Finish and assemble.** Several light coats of a gloss acrylic spray sealer will protect this dipped and painted wind chime. Follow the directions on the can, allowing each coat to dry before applying the next coat. For my gourd, I chose to add a large, 20mm glass foil turquoise bead, a modeling clay disc clapper (see page 57), and a tassel of ³⁄₁₆" (0.5cm)–wide silk ribbon.

Drip Wind Chime

Simple drips, layered from pale to dark color tones, adorn this fun wind chime. A light splattering adds just a touch of sparkle at the top of the gourd.

Supplies

- 4" (10cm) high, 4" (10cm) diameter, 12" (30.5cm) circumference kettle gourd
- Sea sponge
- Wax-coated paper plates
- Small wax-coated paper cups
- Clean water
- Plastic teaspoons
- 2 plastic straws
- Bamboo kitchen skewer
- Scissors
- Latex gloves
- Large, disposable plastic drinking cup
- Toothbrush
- Newspaper (to cover work area)
- Acrylic spray sealer
- Acrylic craft paint:
  - Titanium white
  - Medium bright green
  - Pale yellow cream
  - Medium yellow
  - Bright yellow
  - Bright orange
- 18-gauge copper wire
- Flush cutters
- Straight-nosed pliers
- Round-nosed pliers
- Assorted beads, tassels, and air-dry modeling clay for the clapper decoration

Applying the Sponge Base Coat

1 **Prepare the gourd.** Clean, cut, and sand a small kettle gourd into a wind chime base. Place several teaspoons of medium bright green and titanium white on the paint palette. Double-load a sea sponge with titanium white and medium bright green, following the instructions on page 60. With the green edge of the sponge along the bottom edge of the wind chime, tap the sponge around the base of the wind chime.

2 **Paint the gourd.** Cover the entire gourd with paint, keeping the green near the base. Reload the sponge as necessary for full, blended coverage. Allow to dry.

Dripping and Splattering

3 **Prepare to drip.** Place two teaspoons of pale yellow cream paint in a small paper cup. Add two teaspoons of clean water and mix well. To make the dripping process super easy, set the gourd on top of a tall plastic cup on a wax-coated paper plate throughout the dripping and splattering process.

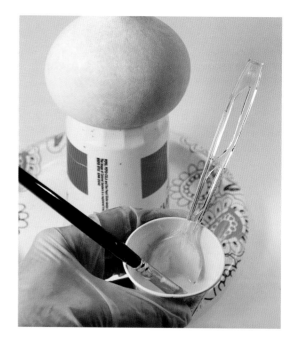

4 **Pick up color.** Cut a plastic straw in half. Dip the straw straight down into the paint and water mix. Place your finger over the open end of the straw. This will trap the color mix inside the straw.

5 **Drip on the first color.** With your finger still over the straw hole, move the straw to the wind chime. Place the bottom hole of the straw about 1" (2.5cm) from the top of the gourd. Remove your finger from the straw hole to allow the paint inside the straw to flow out onto the gourd. Repeat until you have dripped pale yellow cream around the entire gourd.

6 **Release excess paint drops.** Use a bamboo kitchen skewer to release any heavy drops of paint that puddle at the bottom of the gourd.

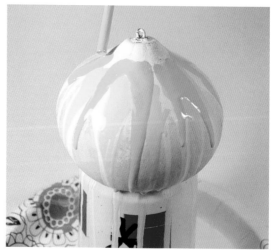

7 **Drip on the second color.** Mix two teaspoons of medium yellow paint in a small paper cup. Add two teaspoons of water and mix well. Drip this color over the pale yellow cream drips you just made.

8 **Drip on the third color.** Mix two teaspoons of bright yellow paint in a small paper cup, add two teaspoons of water, mix well, and drip the gourd with this color in the same manner.

9 **Splatter on a new color.** Mix two teaspoons of bright orange paint with two teaspoons of water and mix well. With a toothbrush, splatter the top one-third of the gourd. (See page 63 for more details on the splattering technique.)

10 **Add one more set of drips.** Load a plastic straw with the bright orange mix and create a final ring of drips around the gourd. Release any heavy drops of color that form at the bottom with a bamboo skewer. Allow the gourd to dry thoroughly.

Finishing

11 **Finish and assemble.** Several light coats of a gloss acrylic spray sealer will protect this dripped and splattered wind chime. Follow the directions on your can of spray, allowing each coat to dry before applying the next coat. For my gourd, I chose to add a large, 20mm glass foil green bead, a modeling clay disc clapper (see page 57), and a rope tassel.

Drip Flowerpot

I enjoyed my creative session making the Drip Wind Chime (page 68) so much that I grabbed a prepared medium cannon gourd to continue the dripping fun. By preparing your dripping colors in advance and working this technique while each color has just been dripped and is still wet, you can create a wonderfully blended gourd art background.

Supplies

- 7" (18cm) high, 7" (18cm) diameter, 21" (53cm) circumference cannon gourd
- Painter's tape
- Wax-coated paper plate
- Small wax-coated paper cups
- Small bowl to hold the gourd
- 2 plastic straws, cut in half
- Plastic teaspoons
- Acrylic craft paint:
  - Black
  - Medium turquoise
  - Bright yellow
  - Pale yellow
  - Pale yellow cream
- Finely ground glitter in silver, black, and bright orange
- Acrylic spray sealer

Creating a Reed Rim

If you want, you can add a reed rim to your project, as I have done for this flowerpot. Just about any rim finish that is used on flat or willow reed baskets can be worked on your gourd art. Do an Internet search for basket rim videos to discover how you can create fantastic rim designs. To prepare a gourd for a reed rim, after cleaning it and creating the opening, drill a series of ⅛" (0.3cm) holes about ½" (1cm) down from the opening, spaced about ½" (1cm) apart. Then weave the rim following whatever technique you choose.

Preparing the Gourd

1 **Apply the base color.** Apply two to three light coats of black paint to the entire outside gourd surface. Allow each coat to dry before working the next coat.

2 **Protect the rim.** If you have added a reed rim to your project, lay strips of painter's tape on it to protect the rim and the inside of the gourd from being colored during the splattering steps.

Dripping

3 **Drip the first color.** Mix two teaspoons of medium turquoise paint with three teaspoons of water in a wax-coated paper cup. Follow the technique on page 71 to begin dripping the color onto the gourd. Move on to the next step while this layer of dripping is still fresh and damp to allow each new layer to mix and blend with the previous one.

For this project, we have used a straw to move the color from the mixing cup to the gourd; that straw makes a narrow, long drip pattern. Try the same technique using a plastic mixing spoon instead. Slowly dribble color from the spoon across the gourd's surface in short, diagonal movements to create a different dripping pattern.

4 **Check your work.** Because this is a thinner mixture than used in the Drip Wind Chime project (page 68), some of the background black coloring will show through the dripping color.

5 **Drip the second color.** Repeat the dripping process using bright yellow. Place the new drips inside the medium turquoise drips from the previous step.

> Because the layer underneath is still wet, each new layer of dripping pushes against the layer below, causing the colors to bleed into each other.

6 **Drip the third color.** Work a third dripping series using pale yellow. Again, place these new drips inside the previous drips.

7 **Drip the fourth color.** Work the fourth layer of dripping using pale yellow cream.

Adding Glitter

8 **Add the first glitter color.** While the last layer of dripping color is still wet, lightly sprinkle the top of the drips with fine silver glitter. The glitter will stick to the wet paint, so you will not need glue or adhesive to anchor it to the gourd.

9 **Add the second glitter color.** Add a light layer of fine black glitter over the wet drips and previously applied silver glitter.

10 **Add the third glitter color.** Work one more layer with fine, bright orange glitter. Because orange is the complementary color to blue, it gives the vase a little bold contrast.

11 **Add final drips.** Add a few more drips of any color that you have used that you want as dominant shades in the design. I chose to re-drip with medium turquoise.

Finishing

12 **Allow to dry.** Let the gourd sit for about half an hour to allow the drips to begin drying. Remove the gourd from the small bowl and set it directly onto a clean paper plate to complete the drying process. At this stage I painted my reed rim with black paint to make the drip design the dominant feature of the flowerpot.

13 **Finish.** Finish the gourd with several light coats of acrylic spray sealer.

Dab Wind Chime

You can use low-tack painter's tape as a masking agent over color work that you have already created in your gourd art. In this project, we will dab the paint colors to create the background coloring. After this has thoroughly dried, painter tape strips will protect some of that background work from an application of solid color, creating a window or striped effect.

Supplies

- 4" (10cm) high, 4" (10cm) diameter, 12" (30.5cm) circumference kettle gourd
- Large ox-hair flat shader brush
- Painter's tape
- Utility knife or bench knife
- Cutting mat or plastic breadboard
- Permanent marker
- Wax-coated paper plates
- Clean water
- Plastic teaspoons
- Scissors
- Latex gloves
- Toothbrush
- Newspaper (to cover work area)

- Acrylic spray sealer
- Acrylic craft paint:
  - Pale yellow
  - Bright yellow
  - Bright orange
  - Pale yellow cream
  - Pale green
  - Medium turquoise
- 18-gauge copper wire
- Flush cutters
- Straight-nosed pliers
- Round-nosed pliers
- Assorted beads, tassels, and air-dry modeling clay for the clapper decoration

Painting with Dabs

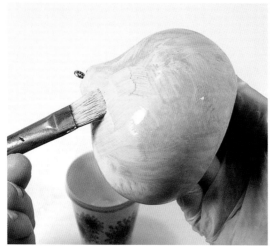

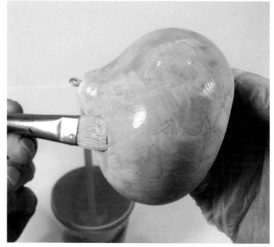

1 **Dab the first color.** Begin by applying one light coat of pale yellow paint to the entire outside of the gourd using a large flat shader brush. Lay the brush against the gourd and then pull slightly. Slowly lift the brush off the gourd, leaving a square-shaped brushstroke. This coat does not need to be fully opaque; let the brushstrokes show.

2 **Dab the second color.** While the pale yellow paint is still damp, fill a large flat shader brush with bright yellow paint. Concentrate your brushwork with this color on the top two-thirds of the wind chime.

3 **Dab the third color.** While the pale yellow and bright yellow paint are still wet, dab bright orange paint onto the gourd. Place these strokes on the top half of the gourd.

You can use any style of brush to create a dab effect. For this wind chime, I used a stiff-bristled ox-hair brush that shows strokes from individual hairs. Experiment on the paint palette with the different large brushes you have in your kit. Try a large, soft-bristled brush, a fan brush, and even a #10 to #12 round brush.

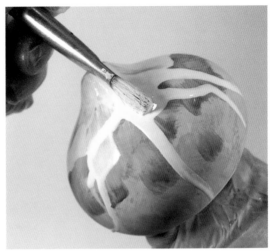

4 **Dab the fourth color.** In the top third of the wind chime, dab pale yellow cream paint. Because we are working wet on wet, the brushstrokes of each new color blend with the color work below them. Dabbing creates wonderful, petal-like strokes.

5 **Drip the fourth color.** Add a little water to the remaining pale yellow cream on the palette and mix well. Load the large flat shader brush fully with color. Lay one side of the brush against the gourd and push to cause the thinned paint to drip down the side of the wind chime.

Adding Stripes

6 **Draw the stripes.** Cut five to six strips of painter's tape that are about 2" (5cm) longer than the circumference of the gourd. Lay the strips on a cutting mat or on a plastic breadboard. With a marker, draw guidelines along the full length of the tape strips in a varying wave pattern.

7 **Cut the strips.** With a craft knife or bench knife, cut along the guidelines to free the wavy strips. Remove the excess tape.

8 **Apply the strips.** Lay the strips of tape onto the gourd, allowing space between each new strip. The spaces between the strips will be painted; the areas covered by the strips will protect the dab background.

9 **Modify the stripes.** With a bench knife or craft knife, you can cut patterns inside of the tape strips to allow even more of the background work to show through the stripes.

10 **Color between the strips.** Place some pale green paint on the palette. With a flat shader brush, apply one to two coats evenly over the areas between the painter's tape strips.

11 **Color along the top of the strips.** Load the brush with pale green. Pull the brush along the top painter's tape strip, allowing the brushstroke to go about ⅛" (0.3cm) beyond the strip. Let the gourd dry until the pale green has lost all of the shine, for about 10 minutes.

12 **Remove the strips.** Gently remove all of the tape strips to reveal the final stripe effect. You can use a damp brush to lift any pale green paint that slipped under the edge of the tape.

Finishing

13 **Splatter the gourd.** Place a small amount of medium turquoise paint on the paint palette. With a toothbrush, splatter the gourd with a light layer of turquoise dots. (See page 63 for more details on the splattering technique.)

14 **Finish and assemble.** Several light coats of a gloss acrylic spray sealer will protect this dripped and splattered wind chime. Follow the directions on your can of spray, allowing each coat to dry before applying the next coat. For my gourd, I chose to add a large, 20mm round green bead with smaller bead accents, a modeling clay disc clapper (see page 57), and a rope tassel.

Dab Pitcher

We will be dabbing, dripping, and splattering a bright, faux-texture background of blues, purples, and pinks to create a vivid, watery effect on this acrylic paint and colored pencil goldfish. As you work this project, you will see that we have brought all of the smooth background techniques used in the previous projects into one project.

Supplies

- 8" (20cm) high, 8" (20cm) diameter, 22" (56cm) circumference cannon gourd
- Two 6" (15cm) high gooseneck gourds
- Superglue
- Acrylic sculpture paste
- Palette knife
- Wax-coated paper plate
- Wax-coated paper cups
- Large, disposable plastic drinking cup
- Tinfoil
- Sea sponge
- Used latex gloves
- Crumbled kraft paper
- Toothbrush
- Painter's tape
- Utility knife or bench knife
- Self-healing cutting board
- Pen
- #2 to #6 graphite pencil
- Liquid mask
- Dishwashing soap
- Reworkable spray sealer
- #6 to #20 red sable fan brush
- #2 to #6 red sable round brush
- #2 to #4 red sable flat shader brush
- #2 to #4 red sable liner brush
- Acrylic craft paint:
    - Matte white primer
    - Pale blue
    - Medium blue
    - Pale purple
    - Magenta
    - Purple
    - Hot pink
    - Dark blue
    - Titanium white
    - Bright yellow
    - Pale orange
    - Bright orange
    - Medium gray
    - Medium brown

Assembling the Pitcher

1 **Make the spout.** Cut a 6" (15cm) high gooseneck gourd around the center line of its wide, bulb-like base. Cut the gourd again at an angle, just above where the neck comes out of the base. This piece will become the spout of the pitcher. Lay the cleaned, cut spout into position on the rim of the cannon gourd. Pencil a guideline along the bottom edge of the spout on the cannon gourd. On the cannon gourd, inside the spout guideline, cut a dip in the gourd rim to allow liquids to flow smoothly out of the pitcher. Allow about ¾" (2cm) of space between this cut dip and the spout's guideline. Drill three ⅛" (0.3cm) holes in the ¾" (2cm) space to become the draining holes for tea leaves (visible in the following photo).

2 **Attach the spout.** Clean, sand, and dry fit the spout to the main gourd. Secure it into place using superglue or sculpture paste.

3 **Secure the spout.** Add several extra drops of superglue or small dabs of sculpture paste along the outside joint of these two pieces.

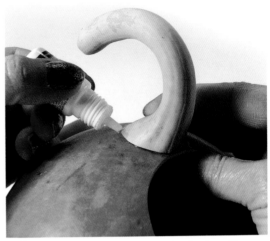

4 **Prepare the handle.** Mark a guideline along the second 6" (15cm) high gooseneck gourd where the neck of the gourd will join the main gourd as a handle. Cut, clean, and sand the handle piece.

5 **Attach the handle.** Dry fit the handle and make any adjustments that are necessary. Use a few drops of superglue or dabs of sculpture paste inside and outside to secure the handle to the main gourd.

6 **Apply sculpture paste.** Place a small amount of sculpture paste onto a wax-coated paper plate or piece of tinfoil. Add a few drops of water if necessary and mix well. Use a palette knife to lift small amounts of paste from the palette and push the paste into the joints of the pitcher. You can also use a large #8 to #12 ox-hair flat shader brush to apply the paste.

7 **Smooth the sculpture paste.** Dip your finger into clean water, and rub and smooth out the sculpture paste both at the joint areas and along the edge line of the paste.

8 **Sand the sculpture paste.** Sculpture paste needs to dry well before you work the sanding steps, usually overnight. Note that the longer it dries, the harder the paste becomes. Sculpture paste allowed to dry over several days can become too hard to sand smooth. When it has sufficiently dried, sand it smooth so that the paste transitions nicely to the gourd.

Painting the Background

9 **Apply primer.** Brush two to three smooth coats of matte white acrylic primer on the outside of the pitcher, including the spout and handle. Allow the primer to dry well, then lightly sand with 220-grit sandpaper for a pristine working surface.

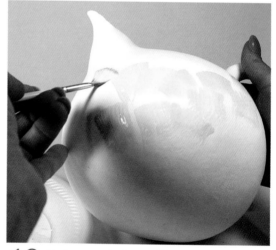

10 **Dab on pale blue.** Place two teaspoons of pale blue paint onto the palette. Load a damp #6 to #10 fan brush with the color. Dab the pale blue all over the pitcher by touching the fan brush tip to the gourd, then lightly pressing it down against the surface. Lift the brush straight up to create triangular brushstrokes, or pull slightly to create square brushstrokes. Allow some of the white primer to show through this coating.

11 **Dab on medium blue.** Repeat step 10 using medium blue paint, working right over the damp pale blue paint. Avoid painting the spout, handle, and about ¾" (2cm) from the top edge of the gourd with this coat. Again, allow some of the background color to show.

12 **Dab on pale purple.** Place about two teaspoons of pale purple onto the palette. Load a fan brush with the color, then touch just the tip of the brush to the gourd. You can lightly roll the brush in your fingers to create a half-circle brushstroke. Apply this layer of color all over the gourd up to about 1" (2.5cm) from the pitcher's rim.

13 **Pat on magenta.** Place a teaspoon of magenta onto the palette. Pat either a sea sponge or a used latex glove crumbled tightly into the magenta. Then pat the paint onto the gourd. Work this layer in the same general area as the pale purple from the previous step.

Just about anything that will accept a layer of acrylic color can be used as a texture stamp: crumpled, dry paper towels, crumpled brown kraft paper, well-used sandpaper, used latex gloves, and even the tangerine bag mesh netting that is used in the Netting Bird project (page 112).

14 **Drip on purple.** Turn the pitcher over and rest it on a large plastic cup. Mix one teaspoon of purple paint with a half teaspoon of water in a wax-coated cup. Pour the mix over the bottom of the gourd to create long drips. You can tilt the gourd on the large plastic cup to make the drips fall diagonally over the body of the pitcher.

15 **Splatter.** With a toothbrush, splatter the entire pitcher with a light coat of hot pink, then with a light coat of magenta. (See page 63 for more details on the splattering technique.) Concentrate the splattering in a thick layer as you work from the top edge of the pitcher to the bottom.

16 **Cut and apply painter's tape strips.** Cut several long strips of painter's tape and lightly lay them on a cutting mat. With a utility knife or bench knife, cut a thick to thin wave pattern along each strip. Lay the center of one piece of tape at the bottom joint of the spout and main gourd. Gently press the tape wave around the gourd until the two sides meet at the back of the gourd. Cut off the excess tape. Repeat to create two more tape waves below the first.

17 **Adjust the strips as needed.** You can cut small pieces of painter's tape wave to match the two ends of the larger pieces of tape. The tape will have wrinkles where it needs to fold to fit the round shape of the gourd.

18 **Pat on hot pink.** Thin the hot pink paint that remains on the palette with water, about half and half. Load a sea sponge with the mix and lightly sponge a layer of hot pink to the top of the pitcher, above the first painter's tape wave.

19 **Pat on dark blue.** Working in the same manner as the previous step, apply dark blue paint to the bottom section of the pitcher, below the last painter's tape wave.

20 **Paint on white.** Brush two coats of titanium white paint over the two spaces created by the painter's tape waves. You will see some of the color work below the white showing through this application.

21 **Remove the painter's tape.** Allow all of the background work to dry for about 15 to 20 minutes. Remove the painter's tape. You can clean up any paint that has bled under the tape edges with the edge of a damp brush.

Painting the Fish

22 **Transfer the patterns.** Make a copy of the two fish patterns (pages 98 and 99) on printer paper. Cut around each fish, allowing a ½" (1cm) margin. Rub the back of the paper with a soft #2 to #6 graphite pencil. Slice into the background margin of the pattern to allow the paper to fold smoothly onto the gourd. Use painter's tape to secure and trace the pattern lines with an ink pen.

23 **Apply a liquid mask.** Place a few drops of dishwashing soap in a small bowl of water. Dampen a #6 to #8 round brush in the soapy water. Blot lightly on a paper towel. The soap will keep the liquid mask from adhering to the brush's bristles. Paint one coat of liquid mask on the background area surrounding the fish patterns to protect the background colors. Let the liquid mask dry until it loses its milky look entirely.

24 **Apply primer.** Apply one light coat of matte white primer to the fish. Allow to dry. Rub your finger over the liquid mask to roll an edge. Grip the edge in your fingers and slowly peel the mask from the gourd. Paint the inside of the pouring spout with titanium white.

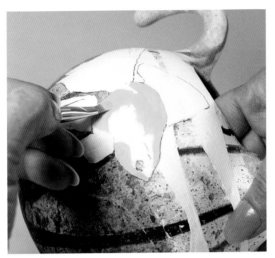

25 **Paint the fish body yellow.** Place a small amount of bright yellow paint onto the palette. Using a small #2 to #4 flat shader brush, apply one coat onto the body of the fish.

26 **Add orange shading.** Working with pale orange and a small flat shader brush, paint one coat of shading on the upper body section, under the top fin, on the front of the belly, and on the top of the head. Work this step while the bright yellow is still damp, and allow the brushstrokes to show.

27 **Add highlights.** Mix a small amount of titanium white with the bright yellow to create a pale yellow. While the previous colors are still damp, highlight along the top of the body: directly under the top fin, on the lower back section of the belly, and along the fish's chin.

28 **Paint the fins.** Place a small amount of bright orange paint onto the palette. Load a #2 to #4 liner brush or use the edge of a #2 to #4 flat shader brush. Pull long orange accent lines onto all of the fins. Start each stroke at the body, pulling toward the outer edge of the fin. Let some of the long strokes overlap to create areas of darker coloring. Add a few drops of medium gray to the white primer to create a pale gray. Shade the fins with long, fine lines, working from the outer edge of the fins toward the body.

29 **Add shading.** On the palette, lay a small amount of medium brown and magenta paint. Mix equal amounts of each to create a brown magenta. Load either a liner or a flat shader, held on its edge, and lay in some shadow lines along the front of the top fin where it touches the body, under each of the gills, along the bottom of the belly, and two lines that flow from the body into the tail.

30 **Add a shadow.** Thin a small amount of the medium brown with water, about half and half. Lightly brush one coat of this mix around the outside of the fish, in the background area, to create a shadow between the fish and the water. Work this step along the sides and bottom of the fish pattern, leaving the top edge of the pattern without a shadow.

31 **Color with colored pencils.** To blend and brighten the fish, add several thin layers of work with artist-quality colored pencils over the acrylic painting. Before doing this, seal the gourd with several light coats of reworkable spray sealer to establish a good surface to color on.

32 **Draw in details.** Use a #2 to #6 graphite pencil to create detailing lines in the fish. You can add a hint of fish scales, create folds in the fins and tail, and accent the top or outer edges of the fins. You can also vary the depth of the graphite gray by using an HD or F graphite pencil in some areas and a #4 or #6 pencil in others.

33 **Add final accents.** With a small #2 to #4 round brush or a #2 to #4 liner brush, add brushstroke spots of bright white on the fish scaling, in the fins and tail, and around the bottom of the eyes. Follow the photos for the placement of these highlights. Add black paint eyes and a few small brushstrokes of pale and medium green leaves in the background. Allow the paint to dry. Finish the gourd with several light coats of spray sealer.

Splatter Birdhouse

While you and I may want brightly colored birdhouses that stand out in our garden, our favorite nesting birds want something that will disappear and blend into the background for the protection of their fledglings. This splattered birdhouse is both. The medium green background helps the gourd hide among the tree leaves, yet the splatter of bright colors will add an attention-getting sparkle and splash.

Supplies

- 7" (18cm) high, 7" (18cm) diameter, 21" (53cm) circumference kettle gourd
- Large, soft-bristled flat shader brush
- #4 to #6 red sable round brush
- #2 to #4 red sable liner brush
- Dishwashing soap
- Liquid mask
- Oil pastels
- Printer paper
- #2 to #6 graphite pencil
- Pen
- Painter's tape
- Toothbrush
- Wax-coated paper plates or tinfoil
- Acrylic spray sealer
- Acrylic craft paint:
  - Medium green
  - An assortment of bright colors in pastel and medium tones: pinks, blues, purples, yellows, and oranges
  - Black

Preparing the Gourd

1 **Apply the base coat and pattern.** Using a large, soft-bristled flat shader brush, apply two to three light coats of medium green paint to the outside of the entire gourd. Allow to dry completely. Make a copy of the leaf patterns (page 105) on printer paper. Rub the back of the paper with a #2 to #4 graphite pencil. Lightly tape the patterns into place, making slices in the background areas as needed to allow the patterns to lie flat against the curved gourd. Trace the design with a pen.

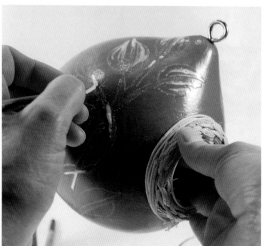

2 **Apply the mask.** Place a few drops of dishwashing soap in a water bowl. Dampen a #4 to #6 round brush in the mix and blot lightly on a paper towel. With the soap-coated brush, apply one coat of liquid mask to the design areas. Wash the brush immediately after use. Allow the mask to dry.

3 **Protect the rim.** I created a reed rim on the opening of my gourd house (see page 74). If you choose to do the same, add a layer of painter's tape to protect it during the painting steps.

You can freehand any pattern onto an acrylic craft paint base coat using an oil pastel. Because the pastel stick is soft, it does not scratch a freshly painted surface like a pencil would. After the painting steps are done, use your finger to simply rub the remaining pastel away.

Splattering

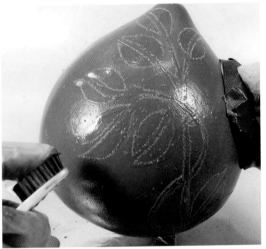

4 **Splatter with the first color.** For each splattering color, place a small puddle of the color on a wax-coated paper plate or tinfoil. Add a few drops of water to lightly thin the color. Load a toothbrush with the first color, medium pink, and splatter the gourd. (See page 63 for more details on the splattering technique.)

5 **Splatter with the second color.** Work a second layer of splattering in pale pink over the entire gourd.

6 **Splatter with cool colors.** Work several more layers of splattering, using blues and purples above the center line of the gourd and greens below the center line.

7 **Splatter with warm colors.** Work several more layers of splattering, using yellows and oranges at the top and bottom sections of the gourd plus some yellow along the center.

8 **Remove the mask.** Allow the splatter work to dry thoroughly. Peel off the liquid mask by rubbing your finger over an edge to lift and roll it off.

Finishing

9 **Paint the design.** Place a small amount of black paint on the palette and, with a #2 to #4 liner brush, fill the pattern area with a solid coating of black. Allow to dry.

10 **Finish.** Once the black paint is dry and you have removed the painter's tape from the basket rim, your birdhouse is ready for two to three light coats of spray sealer.

Leaf patterns
(copy at 135%)

Blown Bird

A plastic straw and some thinned acrylic paint create this delightful artistic background coloring for a copper wire–legged gourd bird. For a visual of how this gourd bird was constructed, see page 41.

Supplies

- 4" (10cm) high, 4" (10cm) diameter, 12" (30.5cm) circumference canteen gourd
- 6" (15cm) high gooseneck gourd
- 3 egg gourds
- 18- to 14-gauge copper wire
- 20-gauge copper wire
- Flush cutters
- Straight-nosed pliers
- Round-nosed pliers
- Hot glue gun and glue or superglue
- 150- and 220-grit sandpaper
- Acrylic sculpture paste
- Plastic straws, cut in half
- Finely ground gold glitter
- Acrylic spray sealer
- Assorted feathers
- Acrylic craft paint:
    - Light tan
    - Burgundy red
    - Bright yellow
    - Bright orange
    - Titanium white
    - Black

Assembling the Bird

1 **Prepare the pieces.** Wash, clean, and cut a canteen gourd following the general preparation instructions. Clean and cut a gooseneck gourd so that one side will attach to the main canteen gourd as a head, neck, and breast area for the bird. Clean and cut one egg gourd in half lengthwise to become the tail section of the bird. Cut the top off of two egg gourds to match the bottom of the main gourd and to become the upper legs. Sand all of the pieces, dry fit, and adjust as necessary. Note that the egg gourd that becomes the tail section has an opening at the top of the bird's body that will later be filled with feathers.

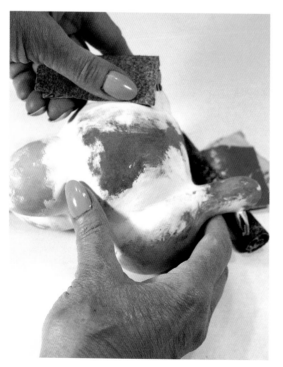

2 **Assemble the bird.** Attach the small gourds to the main gourd using superglue or hot glue. Use sculpture paste to dress out the joints. Create two copper wire legs using 14-gauge copper wire for the center wire lengths and 20-gauge copper wire for the leg wrapping. Follow the copper wire leg instructions on pages 35–37 to create and install the legs into the cut egg gourds. Add more sculpture paste to the leg joints. Allow all the sculpture paste to dry and then sand with 220-grit sandpaper. Remove all of the sanding dust with a damp cloth.

Painting

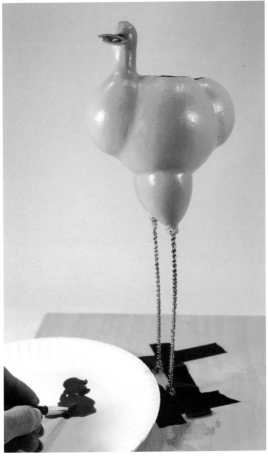

3 **Paint the base coat.** Prime the bird with two light coats of light tan paint. Allow the paint to dry completely. Place a small puddle of burgundy red paint onto the palette. Mix the color with an equal amount of water. Thin every blowing color in this project this way. You want the paints that you use for blowing to be very thin so that the air from the straw can push them across the gourd's surface.

4 **Drip the first color.** Cut a plastic straw in half lengthwise. Fully load a #6 to #8 round brush with the thinned burgundy red. Drip a generous amount of the color onto the bird, laying the brush near the top, cut edge. Let the color run down the bird's body.

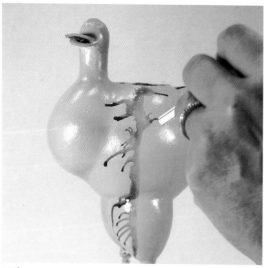 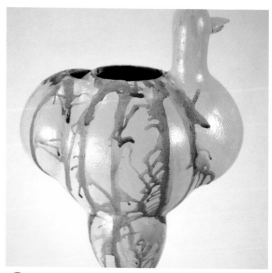

5 **Blow the first color.** Hold the straw close to the color drip and blow gently. The direction in which you hold the straw will determine the direction of the blown fingers of color.

6 **Color the entire body.** Repeat the touch-drip-blow process with the same color until you have worked the color around the entire body of the bird.

7 **Blow the other body colors.** Next, work a layer of bright yellow paint drips, including a drip or two on the bird's head. After that, work a layer of bright orange drips, including a drip or two on the bird's head.

8 **Add the breast coloring.** Add blown drips of titanium white under the bird's chin and on the breast area.

9 **Add glitter.** Sprinkle a light layer of finely ground gold glitter onto the wet drip lines. The wet color will adhere the glitter to the bird without needing a layer of glue. Allow the bird to dry.

10 **Paint the face.** Paint the eyes black by dipping the round end of a brush handle into black paint and then touching the handle to the face of the bird. Paint the beak bright orange. Allow all the paint to dry completely. Seal with two to three light coats of spray sealer.

Finishing

11 **Add the feathers.** Set feathers inside the top hole of the tail egg gourd and hot glue them into place.

Netting Bird

Painting individual feathers can take forever, but you can create the impression of feathers quickly by using a mesh netting as a stencil. As you sponge on layers of color, the mesh protects the area from color application, leaving you with lovely diamond-shaped feathering.

Supplies

- 8" (20cm) high, 8" (20cm) diameter, 22" (56cm) circumference canteen gourd
- 4" (10cm) high bottle gourd
- 8" (20cm) to 12" (30.5cm) square of mesh netting
- 18- or 14-gauge copper wire
- 20-gauge copper wire
- Flush cutters
- Round-nosed pliers
- Straight-nosed pliers
- Superglue or hot glue gun and glue
- Acrylic sculpture paste
- 220-grit sandpaper
- Coarse sea sponge
- Fine sea sponge
- Wax-coated paper plate
- Painter's tape
- Acrylic spray sealer
- Assorted feathers
- Acrylic craft paint:
  - Cream beige
  - Titanium white
  - Pale yellow
  - Bright yellow
  - Pale orange
  - Bright orange
  - Metallic gold
  - Black

Assembling the Bird

1 **Construct the bird.** Wash, clean, and cut a canteen gourd following the general preparation instructions. You will also need a small bottle gourd. Cut the bottle gourd at an angle in the large round section of the bottom of the gourd to become the head, neck, and breast. Glue the bottle gourd to the canteen gourd. Create and attach 5" (12.5cm) copper legs (see pages 35–37) and glue in place. Add a 2" x ¼" (5 x 0.5cm) slit in the top of the back of the main gourd to use for the feathers at the end. Apply sculpture paste at all the joints, allow to dry, and sand with 220-grit sandpaper. Finally, apply two light coats of cream beige paint to the entire construction as a primer. Allow to dry.

Painting the Body

2 **Sponge on a base texture.** Place a large puddle of titanium white paint on the palette. Dampen a sea sponge that has lots of large holes and texturing in clean water. Squeeze out any excess water. Load the sponge with white, tapping the sponge into the puddle of white several times to coat the sponge surface evenly. Press the paint lightly all over the bird body and head in a touch-and-lift motion so that you leave an open-holed pattern with each touch.

3 **Sponge on a second color.** Clean the sponge and reload with pale yellow paint. Apply this color the same way you applied the white.

4 **Sponge on a third color.** Clean the sponge and reload with bright yellow. This color also goes over the back of the bird and the top of his head.

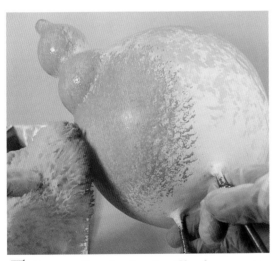

5 **Sponge the chest color.** Check your sea sponges to find a new texture pattern. The sponge I changed to here has a very fine, feathery area that will leave fine, short lines when patted against the bird. Load this sponge with pale orange and work the breast and neck of the bird.

6 **Sponge a second chest color.** Using the same fine-textured sponge, apply a touch-and-lift coat of bright orange to the center area of the breast and neck. Allow the paint layers to dry.

Painting the Feathers

7 **Choose a piece of netting.** Select a piece of orange netting to act as the stencil for making the feather pattern. This piece of orange netting came from a bag of tangerines from the local grocery store.

8 **Color the bird's head.** Place the netting over the head area of the bird. Secure it in place by pulling the lower edges tightly so that the netting is stretched firmly against the gourd's surface. Load the fine-textured sponge with bright orange paint. Tap the sponge several times on the palette to remove any excess paint that could seep under the netting. Then tap the sponge over the netting until the open holes in the webbing spaces are solid orange. Carefully lift the netting off the bird's head.

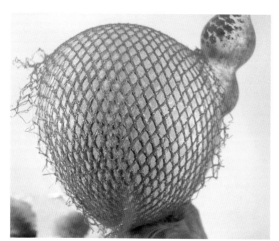

9 **Apply the netting to the bird's back.** Move the netting to the bird's back. Be sure to pull the netting tight so it sits firmly against the gourd's surface.

10 **Color the bird's back.** Load the fine-textured sponge with bright orange. Tap the sponge several times on the palette, then tap the netting area on the back of the bird until all of the netting holes in the top center back are solidly painted. Let the coloring fade or lighten as you work the sponging down the front sides of the bird.

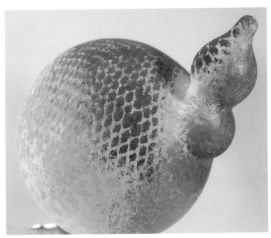

11 **Remove the netting.** Gently lift the netting from the back of the bird. Allow the orange to dry completely.

Finishing

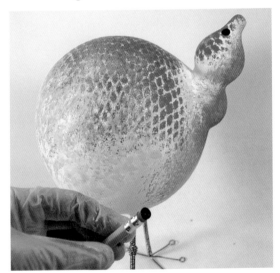

13 **Paint the eyes.** Dip a standard pencil eraser into black paint. Give the bird eyes by touching the pencil eraser against the front of the head. Allow the paint to dry completely, then seal the gourd with two or three light coats of spray sealer.

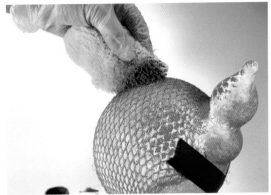

12 **Add another color to the bird's back.** Return the netting to the bird's back. Try to place it in a slightly different position than before so that you don't cover all of the orange during this step. You can use painter's tape to distort the netting, changing the shapes of the holes. Place a puddle of metallic gold paint on the palette. Load the fine-textured sponge with gold and tap it several times on the palette to remove the excess color. Tap the gold on the back of the bird. Remove the netting, position it on the head, and tap a small amount of gold paint there as well. Allow the gold to dry.

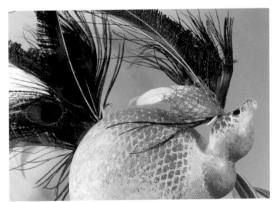

14 **Add feathers.** Your gourd bird is ready for feather decorations. I added a small hole in the top of the head to place a few head feathers there, too. Use hot glue or superglue to adhere the feathers into position. Just for fun, I even added a few small pieces of the mesh netting into the head feathers.

Cloisonné Birdhouse

Cloisonné is the art of capturing or damming enamel paint in between bridges of gold wire on a pottery or metal base. For our cloisonné-effect birdhouse, we will be masking the design so that we can easily apply a dabbed background, then coloring the design with thinned craft acrylics and artist-quality colored pencils. For the wire dams, we will use metallic gold acrylic paint.

Supplies

- 11" (28cm) high, 7½" (19cm) diameter, 23" (58cm) circumference canteen gourd
- 2 egg gourds
- Waxed linen cord
- 220-grit sandpaper
- Printer paper
- #2 to #6 graphite pencil
- Pen
- Painter's tape
- Scissors
- Paper towels
- Liquid mask
- Dishwashing soap
- #4 to #8 red sable round brush
- #10 to #12 stiff-bristled ox-hair flat shader brush
- #10 to #12 red sable flat shader brush
- Reworkable spray sealer
- Paste floor wax finish
- Acrylic craft paint:
  - Matte white primer
  - Medium blue
  - Medium green
  - Medium brown
  - Black
  - Medium purple
  - Bright red
  - Bright orange
- Artist-quality colored pencils in an assortment of shades of yellow, orange, red, green, and purple

Preparing the Gourd

1 Construct the gourd. Wash, clean, and cut a canteen gourd following the general preparation instructions. This gourd is what is used as the example on pages 42 and 43, so if you want to make a fully functional birdhouse, follow those steps as well, including creating a trapdoor, adding ventilation holes, and inserting an eye screw.

2 Add primer. Brush one to two light coats of matte white acrylic primer on the outside of the birdhouse using a large, soft-bristled flat shader brush. Allow to dry.

3 Transfer the pattern. Make a copy of the large flower pattern (page 126) on printer paper. Dry fit the pattern to the curve of the gourd. Rub the back of the paper with a soft #2 to #6 graphite pencil. Mark with a pencil and then cut any place where you can separate or slice the pattern to make it fit as closely as possible against the gourd. Using painter's tape, secure the pattern to the gourd. Trace along the pattern lines with a pen. Remove the pattern from the gourd.

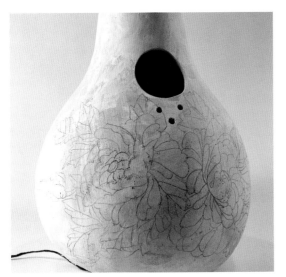

4 **Check the pattern.** Take a few moments to check the tracing for any areas that did not transfer well or need a few lines added for clarity.

5 **Apply liquid mask.** Dip a soft-bristled #4 to #8 round brush in water that has a few drops of dishwashing soap added. The soap will prevent the liquid mask from adhering to the brush's bristles. Brush one even coat of liquid mask over the entire area inside the pattern. Wash the brush immediately. Allow the mask to dry.

Painting

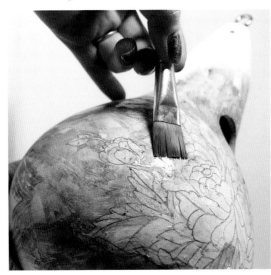

6 **Dab the first color.** The main coloring of this poppy design will be worked in layers of artist-quality colored pencil. But we will be using thinned acrylic craft paint to create the shadow tones upon which those colored pencils will be applied. Start by thinning about two teaspoons of medium blue paint with a half teaspoon of water. With a large, soft-bristled flat shader brush, dab a coating of thinned medium blue on the background areas of the design and along the sides of the design. (See page 82 for more details on the dabbing technique.)

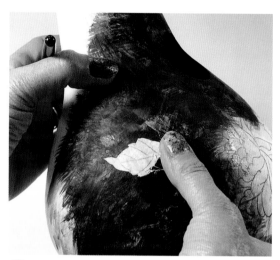

7 **Dab the rest of the colors.** Repeat the background dabbing with thinned medium green, then again with thinned medium brown, and then again with thinned black. You do not need to wait for one color to dry before you begin working with the next.

8 **Remove the mask.** The background should show small, blended areas of each color that you have dabbed onto the gourd. Allow the paint to dry for about half an hour. Then, with your finger, rub from the background into the pattern to roll a small edge of the mask away from the gourd. Grip this roll and peel the remaining mask off the gourd.

My gourd was wide and hard to hold with just one hand, so I worked the background in two stages. I first dabbed the front half of the gourd around the design area. After this area dried, I worked the back half of the gourd, overlapping the front work where the two sections met.

The mottling of this background is very subtle; you will just be able to distinguish the different colors that you applied before you worked the black dabbing. The subtle color changes will help the background areas of the gourd disappear into the tree leaves, giving your favorite backyard nesting birds a wonderful place to hide their nest.

9 **Fix any mistakes.** If you have any small areas of background that were accidentally covered by the mask, you can either use a small brush to dab these areas with color, or you can expand the paint used in that area of the flower design to incorporate it into the painted design work.

10 Start adding the shadow colors.
On a palette, place a small amount of medium blue, medium purple, and bright red. Mix each color about half and half with water. Load a soft-bristled #4 to #6 flat shader brush with the medium blue. Lightly blot the excess color by tapping the brush tip on a paper towel. Paint long shadowing strokes on all of the leaves, working from where a leaf tucks under another element out toward the edge of the leaf. Paint the outer petals of the poppies with purple and the inner petals with bright red in the same manner. (See page 127 for a visual of the completed colors.)

11 Finish adding the shadow colors.
Paint the inner petals in the same manner using bright orange and bright yellow. Add a little accent of red and shadowing to the edges of the leaves and purple to the base of the leaves. (See page 128 for a visual of the completed colors.)

12 Apply reworkable sealer. When the paint has dried, give the entire gourd two light coats of reworkable spray sealer. This will set the thinned acrylic colors, protecting them from the colored pencil points, while providing a light texture on which you can apply colored pencil work.

Coloring with Colored Pencils

13 **Apply the first coat of colored pencil.** Work over the entire design—poppies and leaves—with a medium yellow colored pencil for three to five light coats. Use a tightly packed swirling motion to avoid visible straight pencil lines. Colored pencil art is created by layering extremely thin layers of color, one on top of the other, to slowly develop the coloration of the area. Since these pencil colors are transparent, you can create new colors by laying one color over another. For example, a medium green colored pencil worked over a blue acrylic wash becomes a blue-green color. Adding bright yellow over this mix makes the area a bright yellow green with mid-tone green shadows. As you work, keep your pencil tips sharpened to create the fine, thin lines that blend the best.

14 **Apply more colors.** Begin working bright yellow, bright orange, and bright red colored pencils into the poppy petals. Cover the entire petal with bright yellow, the midsection of the petal back to where the petal tucks under the next element with bright orange, and the painted shadow areas with bright red.

15 **Finish the colored pencil work.** Work the leaves in their entirety first with a bright yellow green, followed by a medium green for the midsections, followed by a deep green for the painted shadow areas. Work the centers in both bright red and magenta purple. Continue adding new layers of colored pencils until you have a richly developed coloration throughout the pattern. When the colored pencil work is complete, give the gourd two light coats of reworkable spray sealer to set the color. Allow the sealer to dry well.

Finishing

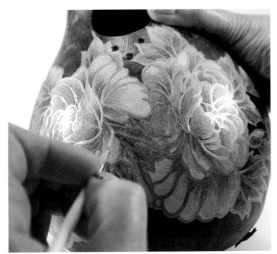

16 **Outline the lines with gold.** Using a #2 red sable liner, outline along all of the pattern tracing lines with gold metallic paint. Use a line that is fairly thick, up to ¹⁄₁₆" (0.2cm) wide. Let the paint dry.

17 **Finish with floor wax.** Finish this piece with a coating of paste floor wax. Floor wax seals the gourd from the rain but still allows the gourd to breathe.

First layer of shadowing

Second layer of shadowing

CHAPTER 3

Textured Projects

IN THE PREVIOUS CHAPTER, we stuck to applying paint directly to the surface of the gourds. In this chapter, we're going to learn how to add much more than paint! We'll create 3D texture using sculpture paste, add textiles and newspaper, and embellish with wire and miscellaneous materials. By the time you've worked through this chapter, you'll be able to sculpt your gourd art into pieces that are both visually and tangibly fascinating.

Throughout the projects in this book, always wash, clean, and cut all gourds following the general preparation instructions before proceeding with the crafting steps. Follow all necessary steps to clean out the insides, protect yourself from dust and mold, and sand edges carefully.

Sculpture Paste Woolly Lamb

With a toothbrush for splattering, wine bottle corks for feet, and a spiral-bend piece of copper wire for fur texturing, this little lamb becomes a guest bathroom accent that is sure to make you smile.

Supplies

- 4½" (11.5cm) high, 6" (15cm) diameter, 18" (46cm) circumference canteen gourd
- 2 egg gourds
- 4¾" (12cm) wide by 1¼" (3cm) tall bottle corks
- Utility knife or bench knife
- Palette knife
- 220-grit sandpaper
- Hot glue gun and glue
- Acrylic sculpture paste
- Several sheets of printer paper
- Wax-coated paper plates
- Newspaper (to cover work area)
- Toothbrush
- Pencil with eraser
- Small round brush
- 8" (20cm) of 18-gauge copper wire
- Flush cutters
- Round-nosed pliers
- Straight-nosed pliers
- 12" (30.5cm) of ½" (1cm)–wide brightly colored ribbon
- 1½" (4cm) gold metallic bell
- Acrylic spray sealer
- Acrylic craft paint:
  - Titanium white
  - Dark gray
  - Navy blue
  - Black
  - Hot pink

Constructing the Lamb

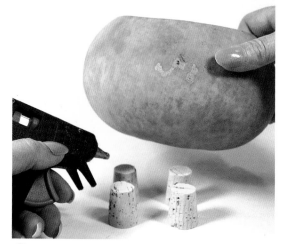

1 Cut the body. Using either a pencil and stack of books, or by dipping the gourd in water, mark a straight, level line along the top of the canteen gourd as a cutting guide. Cut, clean, and sand the gourd.

2 Attach the legs. Place four bottle corks on your work surface with the narrow end up. Dry fit the gourd to the corks to ensure that the cut opening will be level. Adjust the corks' positions as necessary. Hot glue the corks into place. I found it easiest to add the hot glue to the top of all four corks, then set the gourd down onto the corks.

3 Attach the head. This lamb uses two egg gourds: one for the head and one that is cut in half for the ears. Cut one egg gourd to become the head. The cut edge of this small gourd should sit flush against the canteen gourd, just below the cut edge. Hot glue the head into place.

4 **Attach the ears.** Cut two shallow pieces for the ears from the second egg gourd. Add the ears with hot glue, positioned so that the points of the ears point toward the lamb's nose.

5 **Add sculpture paste.** Brush a layer of sculpture paste on the joint between the head and the body. Add a little bit of sculpture paste to the inside joint of the ears and head as well. Smooth all the paste with a damp brush. Allow the paste to dry and then sand with 220-grit sandpaper.

Painting the Body

6 **Add a primer coat.** Place a small puddle of titanium white and dark gray paint onto the palette. Mix the two colors lightly—do not fully blend them together. With a soft-bristled #10 to #12 flat shader brush, apply one to two coats of this primer mix to all of the gourd areas of the lamb. Do not paint the cork legs. As you work, pick up brushfuls of the different color tones in the paint mix. When you are finished, your lamb should have a mottled look.

7 **Prepare for splattering.** As the lamb dries, prepare your area for a splattering session by covering your workspace with newspaper. On a clean area of the palette, place small puddles of white, dark gray, navy blue, and black. Place several sheets of printer paper into the opening of the lamb to protect the inside from the splattering paint.

8 **Splatter the first colors.** Pick up a brushful of dark gray on a toothbrush. Splatter the entire lamb. Because of the way the lamb sits on the worktable, the bulk of the splattering will naturally fall on the upper half of the canteen gourd. Pick up a brushful of the navy blue on the toothbrush. Splatter the entire lamb, concentrating the navy blue on the upper half of the lamb. (See page 63 for more details on the splattering technique.)

9 **Finish splattering.** Splatter the lamb next with titanium white, then with black. Allow all the splatter layers to dry.

Adding the Wool Texture

10 **Make the spiral stamp.** We will be using a spiral stamp made of wire to apply sculpture paste for the curly wool texture. With flush cutters, cut an 8" (20cm) piece of 18-gauge copper wire. Grip the wire end in round-nosed pliers and roll the wire into a loop. Move the loop to straight-nosed pliers and continue rolling the wire into an open spiral for at least two full turns.

11 **Form the stamp handle.** Grip the wire at the end of the spiral and bend the remaining wire at a right angle to create the handle for the spiral stamp.

12 **Test the stamp.** Place a small amount of sculpture paste on the palette. Lightly flatten the puddle with a palette knife. Dip the wire spiral into the sculpture paste lightly so that the bottom of the wire becomes coated with paste. Gently press the wire spiral on a clean area of the palette to check the paste impression the stamp will make. You want a stamp impression that is clearly raised off the palette area and that may have small peaks in the paste. Add a few drops of water to the paste, if necessary, to get the best consistency for stamping.

13 **Stamp the lamb's body.** Stamp the lamb, filling the body with tightly packed sculpture paste spirals. Re-dip the stamp into the sculpture paste for each new spiral. Clean the stamp with water occasionally to remove any paste that has started to dry on the wire.

14 **Stamp the lamb's head.** Add a few spirals to the top of the lamb's head for bangs. Allow all the sculpture paste to dry and harden for about 15 to 20 minutes.

Finishing

15 **Add eyes.** Dip the eraser of a standard pencil into black paint. Gently press the paint-coated eraser against the small egg gourd to create eyes.

16 **Paint the ears and legs.** With hot pink paint and a small round brush, paint the insides of the ears. With dark gray paint and the same brush, paint the four cork legs.

17 **Finish.** Allow the lamb to dry overnight to set the sculpture paste. Seal the lamb with two to three light coats of spray sealer. Tie a gold metallic bell around the lamb's neck using a brightly colored ribbon.

The brown lamb was worked using ochre yellow, beige, and titanium white as the primer mix. She was splattered with medium brown and chocolate brown. Her face and feet were painted using chocolate brown, with hot pink inner ears and black eyes. As a small accent, I hot glued the stem from one of my egg gourds to the back of her canteen gourd to become a tail.

Sculpture Paste Starburst Birdhouse

Acrylic sculpture paste and painter's tape combine to create a simple, geometric, textured starburst pattern. After the paste has dried, wash coats of acrylic craft paint turn the white of the paste into a bright color wheel. This is a great project for gourds that are less than perfect on the surface.

Supplies

- 5" (12.5cm) high, 8" (20cm) diameter, 22" (56cm) circumference canteen gourd
- 30" (76cm) crochet cotton thread
- #2 to #6 graphite pencil
- Painter's tape
- Ruler
- Utility knife or bench knife
- Acrylic sculpture paste
- Wax-coated paper plates or tinfoil
- #6 to #8 red sable flat shader brush
- #6 to #8 ox-hair flat shader brush
- Acrylic spray sealer
- Acrylic craft paint:
    - Bright yellow
    - Bright orange
    - Red
    - Purple
    - Medium blue
    - Bright medium green
    - Titanium white

If you want more of the natural colors of the gourd to show through, don't add white paint in the last step.

Creating the Pattern

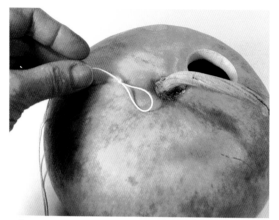

1 Prepare the string. This canteen gourd has a sturdy stem that will serve as the center point of the concentric circles. Using a 30" (76cm) length of crochet cotton or any other heavyweight thread, fold the thread in half and tie a simple knot in the looped end to create a loop large enough to slip over the stem. Then tie knots in the doubled thread at 1" (2.5cm), 2¼" (5.5cm), 3½" (9cm), and 4¾" (12cm) from the center stem loop.

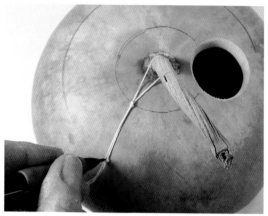

2 Draw the circles. Slide the point of a pencil between the double strings above the 1" (2.5cm) knot. Pull the string tight and move the pencil point around the gourd to draw a circle. The string and pencil act as a compass. Repeat at each knot to draw four circles total.

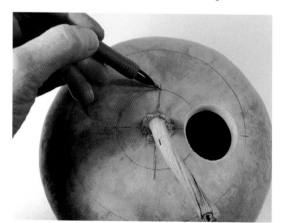

3 Mark four sections. Place your nose directly over the gourd stem. This centers your line of sight on the center of the gourd. Make one mark directly in front of the stem and one directly behind it. Make one mark to the left and one to the right. This divides the gourd into quarter sections.

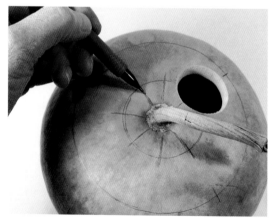

4 Mark eight sections. Continuing with your line of sight centered on the gourd stem, divide each quarter section in half, creating a total of eight equal divisions.

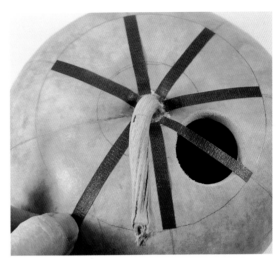

5 **Complete the sections.** Working from the division marks you made at the top, mark the other circles so that each circle is divided into eight sections. Use the string as a guideline if necessary.

6 **Apply the first row of tape.** Lay several long strips of painter's tape onto your cutting mat. With a ruler and utility knife or craft knife, cut the tape into strips that are ¼" (0.5cm) wide. Lay the ¼" (0.5cm) strips of tape along each of the division lines, starting at the stem. Press into place and cut the tape at the guideline for the second circle.

7 **Complete the first row of triangles.** Following the photo, lay a strip of tape connecting the bottom edge of two of the pieces of tape you just placed. Cut the tape to create a triangle shape. Tape along the second circle until all eight units have become closed triangles.

8 **Create the second row of triangles.** Make pencil marks along the third circle line to divide each unit in half. Working from the flat sides of the triangles you have already created, create a new row of triangles with the tape.

9 **Make a zigzag line.** Make a zigzag pattern with the tape ¼" (0.5cm) down from the second row of triangles.

10 **Create the diamonds.** Turn the zigzag row into a series of diamonds by closing off the bottom angle of each zigzag point by carrying the taping pattern down to the last pencil circle.

Applying the Paste

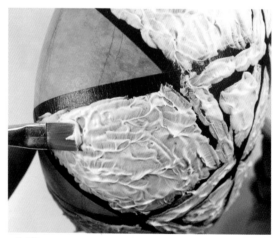

11 **Prepare the sculpture paste.** Place sculpture paste onto a wax-coated paper plate or sheet of tinfoil. Add a few drops of water, thinning it just enough so that you can easily manipulate it with a #6 to #8 flat shader brush. Pick up a small amount of paste on the end of a flat shader brush. Apply the paste inside a triangle. Tap lightly to create heavily textured peaks in the paste.

12 **Fill the shapes with sculpture paste.** Fill all the triangles, the space between the zigzags, and all the diamonds. Leave the bottom area uncovered.

13 **Remove the tape.** Allow the sculpture paste to dry for a few minutes, but not completely set. Then remove the painter's tape.

14 **Fix any mistakes.** You can use a damp #6 to #8 flat shader brush to wash away any sculpture paste that was able to get under the painter's tape. Allow the paste to dry completely by setting it aside for the night.

Painting

15 **Paint the sculpture paste.** On a palette, place a small amount of each of the following colors: bright yellow, bright orange, red, purple, medium blue, and bright medium green. Brush one coat of each color onto the gourd, following the photo for placement. To create a blended effect, apply one color next to another while each color is still wet.

16 **Paint white lines.** Using titanium white, paint one to two coats over all the tape lines above the purple zigzag line. Allow the paint to dry thoroughly, and then seal with two to three light coats of spray sealer.

Textile Birdhouse

Any natural fiber material can easily be collaged to the surface of a gourd using archival white glue. This fun birdhouse uses paper coffee filters, cotton cheesecloth, burlap, garden twine, and cotton cord to create a riot of texture. When the collage work is dry, oil pastels add bright color to the high ridges of the texture.

Supplies

- 10" (25.5cm) high, 8" (20cm) diameter, 23" (58cm) circumference kettle gourd
- #2 to #6 graphite pencil
- Wax-coated paper cups
- Archival white glue
- Plastic mixing spoon
- Bowl of water
- #6 to #12 ox-hair flat shader brush
- Latex gloves
- Coffee filters
- Cheesecloth
- Burlap
- Assorted string, cords, and twine
- Scissors
- Acrylic craft paint in dark brown
- Set of 12 to 24 oil pastel sticks
- Acrylic spray sealer

Applying the Fabrics

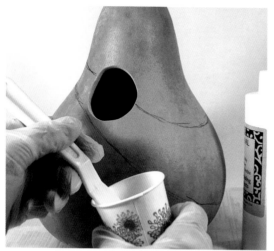

1 **Divide the gourd.** Divide the outside of the gourd into three sections, using a pencil to create the guidelines. The top section will be worked with coffee filters, the second section with cheesecloth, and the bottom section with burlap. In a wax-coated paper cup, mix three tablespoons of archival white glue and one tablespoon of water.

2 **Wet a filter.** Put on latex gloves. Work with one coffee filter at a time. Dip a filter into clean water, then wring out any excess water. You want the filter damp but not dripping.

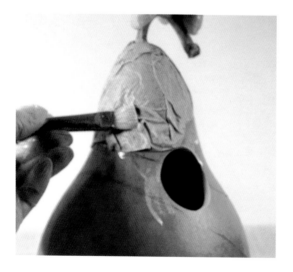

3 **Apply the filter.** With a large flat shader brush, apply one coat of the glue mix to the top section of the gourd. Place the filter onto the glue and press it firmly in place with the brush.

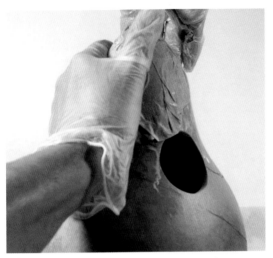

4 **Apply more glue.** Apply more glue to the filter with the brush as necessary to secure the filter in place. Use the palm of your hand to press the thickest wrinkles into place.

5 **Add more filters.** Working with one filter at a time, cover the entire top section of the gourd. Overlap the filters to avoid empty spots. When you have completely covered the top section with filters, brush one coat of the glue mixture over the entire area.

6 **Apply cheesecloth.** Mix more archival white glue and water if you are running low. Cut a piece of cheesecloth into small 3" (7.5cm) to 4" (10cm) squares. You can work several overlapping layers of cheesecloth at a time to increase the texture for this area. Dip the cheesecloth squares in clean water, then blot well on paper towels. Brush a coat of the glue mixture on the central area of the gourd. Place several layers of cheesecloth onto the glued area and use a brush to press the pieces into place.

7 **Apply burlap.** The bottom section of the gourd is covered with 3" (7.5cm) squares of burlap. Dampen and blot the burlap pieces on a paper towel. Coat the bottom section of the gourd with the glue mix. Lay one piece of burlap onto the gourd and apply a second coat of glue mix over the burlap. Continue working along the pencil line for this section, overlapping each new burlap piece over the last piece applied. Work just one ring of burlap pieces along the bottom.

8 **Allow to dry.** Allow all the layers to thoroughly dry. Visual contrast is important when you want to artistically emphasize texture. The unworked bottom area on this birdhouse gives the eye an area of smooth gourd surface to compare to the textures you have created.

Applying the Strings

9 **Choose a variety of strings.** Gather a variety of cotton and twine strings and cords. While you can use just one type of string, using a variety adds to the textured effect of this collage.

10 **Attach the first string.** Wrap a long piece of twine around the gourd. Move the twine to an intersection between two of the textured areas. Tie a square knot and cut the excess twine from the knot to about 1" (2.5cm) long. Brush a generous coat of the glue mix to the twine to hold it in place. The twine wrapping does not have to fall precisely on the joint between the two different textures; let it fall naturally.

11 **Attach more strings.** Add more strings, cords, and twine, placing the knots for each in a line down the front of the gourd. Let the strings go over the birdhouse hole as you add them. Glue the strings down, including the areas that are over the hole. After the glue has dried overnight (in the following step), you can cut the small sections of the string that cover the hole without affecting the string at the sides of the hole.

12 **Finish gluing the strings.** Let the gourd dry for about an hour, then apply one more coat of the glue and water mix to all of the textured areas. Dry overnight. Even though the glue is well dried, it will have a slightly tacky feeling. This will diminish with the spray sealer step at the end of the project.

Applying Color

13 **Apply a base coat.** Place two teaspoons of dark brown paint into a wax-coated paper cup. Add half a teaspoon of water and mix well. Brush this mix on the entire outside of the gourd and allow it to dry completely. The thinned color will not give full, solid coverage. Instead, it will create light and dark areas of brown, depending on the texture in the area.

14 **Color with pastels.** Using one oil pastel stick at a time, rub a color over one of the textured areas. The pastel will adhere to only the highest areas of the texture, leaving the deep, dark brown painted areas untouched. Although not shown in this project, you can blend oil pastels by laying one color over another lightly. This lets a little of both colors show and creates a new, blended color.

15 **Fix any mistakes.** You can clean off any pastel color that has gotten into the wrong area by simply rubbing the area with your fingers.

16 **Color the strings.** Use contrasting colors for the strings by rubbing the oil pastel stick along the top edge of each string. Finish this birdhouse with two to three light coats of spray sealer.

This color wheel mobile is created using egg gourds that have had the bottom cut and opened. Follow the general directions for the Textile Birdhouse, using paper coffee filters for the top half of each egg gourd and cheesecloth for the bottom half. Tie a heavy cotton cord along the joint line between the coffee filters and cheesecloth. Add the last layer of glue mix and let dry overnight. Base coat the textured gourds with black paint and let dry. The oil pastels are applied in a repeat pattern: the color used on the bottom cheesecloth area of the top gourd is repeated on the coffee filter top of the next gourd, etc. White oil pastel was used on all of the strings. Create copper wire hanging loops to attach the hanging strings. I wrapped an 8″ (20cm)-wide embroidery hoop with raffia for the hanger. You could also hang this group of gourds from a twisted grapevine branch.

Crochet Bowl

One of my evening hobbies is thread crochet, working those old-fashioned lace doilies that our grandmothers made. A line of four square tablecloth motifs became a perfect accent for this cannon gourd. While I used a handcrafted crochet motif, you might also use lace and burlap ribbon, cotton lace trim, or cotton braiding—any natural fiber sewing trim can become a gourd accent.

Supplies

- 6" (15cm) high, 8" (20cm) diameter, 22" (56cm) circumference cannon gourd
- Four 4" (10cm) square cotton thread crocheted motifs (or similar)
- Archival white glue
- Latex gloves
- Sea sponge
- Acrylic spray sealer
- #10 to #12 stiff-bristled flat shader brush
- #10 to #12 soft-bristled flat shader brush
- Terry cloth towel
- Paper towels
- Acrylic craft paint:
  - Metallic gold
  - Navy blue
  - Black

1 **Attach the motifs.** Dip the crochet motifs in a bowl of clean water. Drain them, then blot them heavily on a dry terry cloth towel. You want the cotton slightly damp so that it pulls the glue mixture into the cotton thread fibers. Mix three teaspoons of archival white glue with one and a half teaspoons of water. Stir well. This is a thin, watery solution. Wearing latex gloves, dip the motif into the mixture and fully saturate it. Remove the motif from the glue mix and let the excess glue drip off. Place the glue-soaked motif into position on the gourd and press into place. Wipe any glue drips off the gourd with a damp paper towel. With a damp, stiff-bristled flat shader brush, work out any puddles of glue that form between the open sections in the motif. Apply all four motifs, then allow the piece to dry overnight.

2 **Paint with gold.** Using a soft-bristled #10 to #12 flat shader brush, apply two even coats of metallic gold acrylic paint to the entire outside of the gourd, including the crochet motifs. Allow to dry.

3 **Paint with navy blue and black.** Place a small puddle of navy blue paint onto the palette. Thin lightly with a few drops of water. Paint one even coat of navy blue on just the crochet motifs and the exposed gourd inside of the motifs. Brush over the navy blue with a clean, lightly damp brush to smooth out any puddles that may have formed inside the strings. Allow to dry for a few minutes. Then repeat this process using black paint to give the crochet areas an antiqued look.

4 **Adjust the paint.** With a damp sponge, wipe off the high areas of the crochet motifs. This will remove some of both the navy and black paint from the top of the motif, making the high areas paler in color that the deeper areas. Allow to dry overnight. Two to three light coats of gloss spray sealer finish this delightful antique-style bowl.

Newspaper Collage Bird

I had finished all the painted practice gourds and project gourds planned for this book. Yet on my worktable, I still had this wonderful copper wire bird gourd and a pile of raw materials—burlap fabric, coffee filters, paper rope, and cotton twine. All my crafting supplies were still set out, too, including archival white glue, sculpture paste, and a hot glue gun. Plus I had a nice pile of old newspapers that had not yet been used to cover my table. So what else could I do but create just one more fun project? This project uses very minimal painting or coloring; instead, it's a newspaper collage that uses all of the gourd art supplies you already have on hand from the previous projects.

Supplies

- 11" (28cm) high, 7" (18cm) diameter, 20" (51cm) circumference kettle gourd
- 1 round egg gourd
- 1 oval egg gourd
- Superglue
- Acrylic sculpture paste
- 220-grit sandpaper
- Archival white glue
- 18- to 14-gauge copper wire
- 20-gauge copper wire
- Newspaper
- Wax-coated paper cups
- Wax-coated paper plate
- 4" x 5" (10 x 12.5cm) piece of lightweight cardboard
- 4" x 6" (10 x 15cm) piece of rusty chicken wire
- 4" x 5" (10 x 12.5cm) piece of burlap
- Small cereal bowl
- Spray adhesive
- Scissors
- Flush cutters
- Hot glue gun and glue
- 20" (51cm) of 2½" (6.5cm)–wide lace-edged burlap ribbon
- 2 pieces of ⅛" x 2" (0.3 x 5cm) cork sheet, or circular cork scrapbooking tags
- Two 14mm disc shell beads
- Rust-colored paper rope
- Paper-coated wire
- 1 yard (1m) of ⅜" (1cm)–wide satin ribbon
- Acrylic spray sealer
- Acrylic craft paint in neutral beige

Constructing the Bird

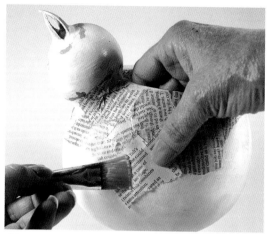

1 **Prepare the bird body.** Create a copper wire gourd bird following the general instructions on pages 33–40. For primer, apply one coat of neutral beige paint over the entire piece. After it dries, sand well with 220-grit sandpaper to remove any brushstroke ridges or small edges from the sculpture paste steps. Wipe any sanding dust from the gourd using a damp cloth.

2 **Start collaging newspaper.** Mix three teaspoons of archival white glue with one teaspoon of water. Tear newspaper into small, random-shaped pieces. Brush a coat of the glue mix on a small area of the bird, and then lay a piece of newspaper onto the glue. Using a brush loaded with the glue mix, press the newspaper firmly against the gourd.

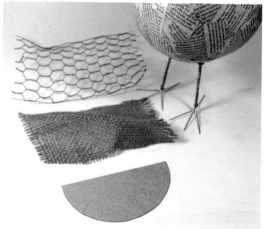

3 **Cover the body with newspaper.** Twist, turn, and invert each new piece of newspaper so that the printing goes in all directions. Overlap each new piece on those already applied for full coverage. Allow the gourd bird to dry overnight.

4 **Cut the wing pieces.** For each wing, you will need a 4" x 5" (10 x 12.5cm) piece of lightweight cardboard, a 4" x 6" (10 x 15cm) piece of rusty chicken wire, and a 4" x 5" (10 x 12.5cm) piece of burlap.

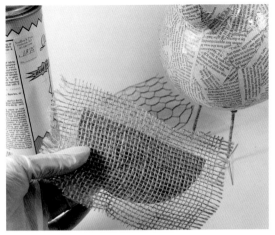

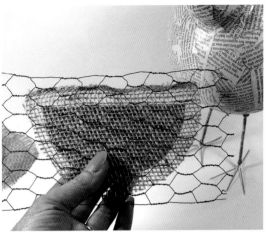

5 **Attach the burlap to the cardboard.** Cut the cardboard into a half-circle by tracing around a small cereal bowl and cutting the cardboard with scissors. Following the directions on the can, apply one coat of spray adhesive to the cardboard. Place the burlap over the adhesive and press it firmly into place. Then trim the excess corners of the burlap, leaving about a 1" (2.5cm) margin of fabric along all the edges.

6 **Place the wire.** Lay the piece of rusty chicken wire over the burlap cardboard wing. Align the wire so that one row of the wire runs evenly across the straight edge of the half-circle wing.

7 **Attach the wire.** Carefully fold over the edges of the chicken wire around to the back of the cardboard. Clip any excess wire with flush cutters. Lay the finished wing face up on your worktable. Lay a book or board on top of the wing and press down firmly to flatten the wing construction as much as possible.

8 **Form the wings.** With a light pressure against the top corners of the burlap wire wings, bend the wings into a gentle cup shape.

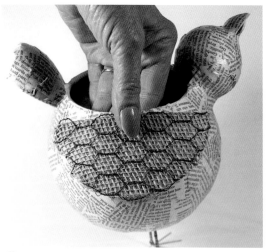

9 Check the wing fit. Place the wing against the gourd to check the shape and to determine exactly where you want to attach the wing. The center top of my wing is level with the cut opening in the gourd.

10 Attach the wings. Use hot glue to hold the wing in place against the bird body. Place the glue drops well inside the wing shape so that the top edge points of the wing stand free from the gourd. Add a few spots of glue along the bottom center of the gourd.

Embellishing the Bird

11 Prepare burlap ribbon. Cut six pieces of 2½" (6.5cm)–wide lace-edged burlap ribbon into 1" (2.5cm) strips. Cut each strip in half.

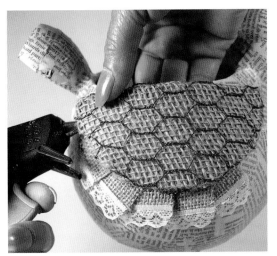

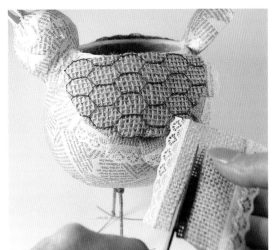

12 **Embellish the wings.** Tuck one cut piece of burlap ribbon under the wing, starting about 2" (5cm) down from the front top corner. Hot glue this piece to the wing, not to the gourd. Tuck the next piece of laced burlap next to the first, overlapping the first by about ¼" (0.5cm). Hot glue this piece to the wing. Continue adding laced burlap feathers until you reach the back top point of the wing.

13 **Prepare ribbon for the tail.** From the same 2½" (6.5cm)–wide lace-edged burlap ribbon, cut a strip that is ¾" (2cm) wide (including the lace) by 3" (7.5cm) long.

14 **Embellish the tail.** Hot glue this strip of burlap ribbon to the tail, working across the width of the tail. After the hot glue cools, cut off any excess ribbon using scissors.

15 **Cut eye shapes.** Using scissors, cut a 1¼" (3cm) circle from ⅛" (0.3cm)–thick cork sheet or from a circular cork scrapbooking tag. Using a small medicine bottle cap, mark a partial circle in the lower half of the cork circle, creating an oval shape. Cut along the marked line and discard the oval, saving the thicker half-moon piece for the bird's eyes. Cut a second half-moon shape from another piece of cork sheet.

16 **Add beads.** Hot glue a large 14mm disc shell bead to the back of each half-moon cork eye to become the bird's pupils.

17 **Prepare paper rope pieces.** Cut about five 3" (7.5cm) pieces of rust-colored paper rope for each eye. Holding one end of a piece of rope in your fingers, unroll the rope just below your fingertips. This creates a tight tip that flows into a flared area of paper with about a 2" (5cm) tight twisted stem. Repeat for all the paper rope pieces.

18 **Glue the paper ropes to the eyes.** Using hot glue, attach the paper rope feathers to the backs of the cork eyes. Angle the paper ropes as you glue them so that the flared areas point toward the opening of the gourd. See the photo for the correct position.

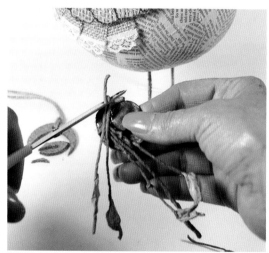

19 **Trim the eyes.** You can cut away any excess paper rope with scissors. Using hot glue on the back of the shell bead, attach the eyes to the bird's head.

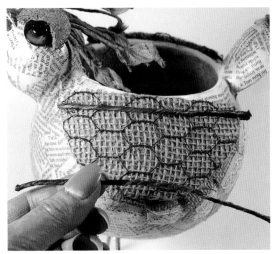

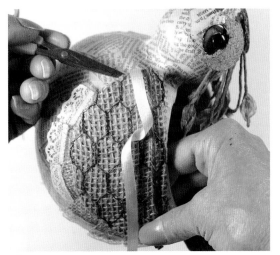

20 **Add paper-coated wire.** With flush cutters, cut a piece of paper-coated wire that is 2" (5cm) longer than the width of the wing. Fold 1" (2.5cm) of wire over on each end using round-nosed pliers. Slide the wire over the wing with the folded ends tucked under the wing. Hot glue the folded portions of the wire to the back of the wing. Repeat for the other wing, and follow the same procedure to add a paper-coated wire to the tail.

21 **Add ribbon.** Cut two 8" (20cm) lengths of ³⁄₈" (1cm)–wide satin ribbon for each wing. Hot glue one end of one ribbon tucked around the back of the wing, just below the paper-coated wire. Hot glue a second piece of ribbon in the same manner to the other side of the wing. Tie the two ribbon pieces together into a simple bow slightly off-center, toward the back of the wing. Trim the excess ribbon ends. Repeat for the second wing bow. Complete this newspaper collage bird with two to three light coats of spray sealer.

Ready to Fly

Hopefully I have provided enough new learning and new techniques that you can go on to create your own artistic designs in your gourd crafting. Now, remember these two little birds from the beginning of the book? You've learned all the skills you'll need to make them yourself without any detailed instructions. But here are the details if you want to make lookalikes.

These two owls were made using egg gourds as the main body. The bottom of the egg gourd was cut to clean out the seeds and so that the body would sit levelly on the pine bark after the project was complete. The eyes were made from cut bottle corks, ¾" (2cm) wide by 1¼" (3cm) tall, and were attached with hot glue; the beaks are glued gourd seeds left over from one of my larger gourds.

The half-circle white chest feathers were worked using a copper wire stamp, just as we used to create the Sculpture Paste Woolly Lamb (page 132). The long wing feathers were created in the same manner using a long, curved piece of copper wire.

The dabbed coloring for the breast, wings, and back was worked just as we dabbed the background colors for the Cloisonné Birdhouse (page 118). Red, orange, and yellow were used on the breast, and golden tan, medium brown, and black were dabbed on the wings and back. While these colors are still damp, you can gently rub a damp cloth over the sculpture paste half-circles to clean them back to white.

The eyes were shaded in bright yellow and bright orange, and the pupils were made using the end of a brush handle dipped in black paint then touched to the cork near the beak. The beak was painted bright yellow.

After adding a few feathers to the tops of their heads, these two little guys are ready to take up their place on your mantel, and you're ready to step out (or fly off!) into a wide world of independent gourd crafting.

About the Author

Internationally known artist Lora S. Irish is the author of more than 30 woodcarving, pyrography, and craft pattern books.

Her books include *Great Book of Carving Patterns*, *World Wildlife Patterns for the Scroll Saw*, *The Art and Craft of Pyrography*, *Relief Carving the Wood Spirit*, *Great Book of Celtic Patterns*, and many more. Winner of the Woodcarver of the Year award, Lora is a frequent contributor to *Woodcarving Illustrated* and *Scroll Saw Woodworking & Crafts* magazines.

Working from her rural mid-Maryland home studio, she is currently exploring new crafts and hobbies, including wire jewelry, metal sheet jewelry, piece patch and appliqué quilting, gourd carving, gourd pyrography, and leather crafts. Visit her at *www.LSIrish.com*.

Index

Note: Page numbers in *italics* indicate projects.